This book was published by Stewed Rhubarb Press
in November 2019, with the ISBN number
978-1-910416-12-9

Performance Rights Agent:
Alan Brodie Representation,
The Paddock Suite, The Courtyard,
55 Charterhouse St, London EC1M 6HA
tel: 020 7253 6226 email: alan@alanbrodie.com

10th Anniversary Editon

Edited by Annabel Cooper & James T. Harding

Typesetting, layout and cover by James T. Harding
www.james-t-harding.com

Publicity by Charlie Roy

Jo Clifford

The Gospel According to

Jesus, Queen of Heaven

10TH ANNIVERSARY EDITION

www.stewedrhubarb.org

Contents

Preface: The Birth of Queen Jesus

by Jo Clifford, writer and performer

This story begins in a church.

A church in an all-male world. It is an English boys' boarding school. There are no girls or women anywhere.

Just men and boys.

And me. I have a strong feeling, which I keep trying and failing to deny, that I am not a boy and will never be a man either. And this shames and terrifies me.

I am playing a girl in a play and I love it. But I am also terrified that people will see how much I love it and will hate me. The bullying and hatred in this supposedly Christian institution is so cruel that I fear I will never survive it.

My mother has died, just over two years ago, and I feel completely alone in the world. I know no-one will help me.

I have just discovered my vocation on the stage but I do not truly know that. The fear and guilt and shame in me is too strong.

All the men and boys are singing a hymn. Probably about being Christian soldiers. I cannot join in. I have been told I cannot sing, and anyway my voice is still high and I am ashamed of it.

So I have no voice. I am silent.

I turn my back on the theatre.

Jesus does not help me. Jesus is part of the institution that silences me.

The story of how I escaped this trauma and this imprisonment is very long. For now, I should say that what rescued me was love. The love of my partner, Susie, and of my children, Rebecca and Katie. They loved me when I could not love myself.

It was with their help that I discovered my voice as a playwright in 1985, after twenty years of trying.

And it was with their help that I became able to heal the deep division within myself and finally become whole.

We shared the children's upbringing, Susie and I. We

divided the week in half. And so half of my time I was their mother as well as their father.

And for the other half of the week, I wrote plays with women at the centre whenever I could. I became the women in my plays and so, bit by bit, we became stronger, me and the woman inside me, until we were strong enough and fierce enough to come out and live authentically in the world.

By my late forties, I was no longer wearing men's clothes. I could not bear to. I did not try to pass as a woman. I just wore earrings and women's tops and trousers, and people complimented me on my taste in clothes.

I tried to write about trans issues in the 90s, but all the plays I wrote about it were turned down and I stopped being a fashionable playwright. In fact, I stopped getting commissions for original theatre plays altogether and had to take a job teaching actors in a university.

I don't know if I taught them anything, to be honest, even though I became a professor. But they taught me so much.

The most important thing I learned from them was that maybe I could perform too. And that was important because I understood that if I wanted to write plays about trans women, I needed to work with trans actresses.

And as far as I could tell, there weren't any.

So I had to perform myself. And I knew, somehow, *that* was important. *That* would help me heal the abuse of the past.

Meantime, I was commissioned to adapt novels, translate plays from French and Spanish, and do everything except pursue my own work.

It became clear that I needed to write something for myself, and that I could not count on Scottish theatre to help me do it. I would need to subsidise it myself.

Luckily, my salary as a university professor helped me to do just that.

The result was *God's New Frock*, which, after a couple of years of research and development, I performed in the Traverse and the Tron in 2003.

I wanted to understand why I hated myself so much for

being trans. Was it to do with my Christian upbringing? How much was this hatred inspired by the Old Testament?

I came to understand that before humanity worshipped the father god high in the sky, we worshipped the mother goddess with her roots in the earth. And that one of the dramas being played out in the Old Testament is the remorseless suppression by the father god of their feminine origins.

I suddenly saw this so clearly in the massive lie propagated by one of the stories of the origin of humanity. The one that says woman came out of man. The one which contradicts the most basic and fundamental truth of human experience and yet which, up to then, I had not noticed was so blatant a lie.

In the play, I told the story of the father god's suppression of his feminine self in parallel with the forced suppression of my own feminine self when I was an adolescent and a child. I came to the conclusion that the Bible is a piece of pornography, because reading it had corrupted and degraded my young and innocent self.

I wondered if people would be offended. But no. No-one seemed to care much. The play sold out, both at the Traverse and the Tron, and I might have celebrated its success if I hadn't had a breakdown half way through the run.

I turned up to work one day and begun crying and couldn't stop. It was as if I could no longer function in the world. I couldn't write; in fact, I thought I would never be able to write again. I assumed I wouldn't be able to perform the show, which was serious because the run in the Traverse was due to begin in a week's time.

But I experimented with saying my lines and going through my moves on the living room floor. To my surprise, I remembered them all. It felt like a ritual that somehow brought me comfort. So the Traverse performances went ahead, and the little circle of light round me on the stage felt like a refuge from the ruins of my life.

I would have been happy to go on performing the play, but my producer came down with meningitis, and my director stopped working in the theatre. And I was in no fit state to find new bookings. So that particular play seemed destined to disappear, and in the turmoil and the trauma of the next few years I literally forgot all about it.

I was preoccupied with trying to translate the impossibly difficult medieval text of the *Celestina* to be put on at the Edinburgh International Festival. I was trying to set up a playwriting masters course in the university where I was professor. I knew that sooner or later I would have to start living as a woman. I was making two plays out of Goethe's *Faust* for Edinburgh's Royal Lyceum.

I invented a character called the Poet who was a man in Part One and a woman in Part Two. And that was how I announced my transition.

I didn't need to invent the character of Mephistopheles, whose existence is devoted to destruction, because he had taken up residence in my partner's brain. Susie was dying of a brain tumour all through the summer and autumn and winter of 2004-5. I looked after her. I looked after my children. I tried to look after myself.

I kept writing. *Celestina* opened in August 2004, just after Susie had been diagnosed. *Anna Karenina* opened in March 2005, just after she had died. *Faust Part One* and *Faust Part Two* opened in April 2006, just before my heart gave under the strain.

God's New Frock reappeared in the middle of this nightmare. Unbeknownst to me, Playwrights' Studio Scotland had sent the play to an Italian company who had chosen it to be part of a season of Scottish plays.

So in June 2005 there I was, a bit bemused, in the Teatro della Limonaia, in Florence, watching the play in Italian. It was a full house. The audience were loving it. Some of the jokes even got a round of applause. I was sitting there, watching it all, still dazed by grief.

A couple of months before, I'd realised I could not bear to go on living as a man. I'd begun to take female hormones and start the formal process of transitioning to living as a woman. But my passport was still male. At home, people were insulting me in the street. I felt bewildered and traumatised, but, somewhere inside all this distress, I understood that a trans take on Bible stories was something people really responded to, and I managed to propose the idea of a New Testament sequel to a theatre company.

Even though I didn't know anything about this new play, *Queen Jesus* was stirring in the unknown darkness. She was preparing to be born.

And then I forgot about her again in the midst of finishing and rehearsing the two Faust plays. Soon after they opened I began to feel afraid. I didn't know what it was I was afraid of, exactly. It was true that, by this stage, I was trying much harder and more consistently to present myself as a woman out on the street, and that I was still getting stared at and shouted at and insulted, but this fear didn't seem connected to that, somehow.

It felt like a state of physical terror. My heart would beat unbearably fast. I would feel nauseous with the fear in the pit of my stomach. I would be in a cold sweat. My legs would seem to have no strength in them. It became impossible to get about, so I went to my doctor, and she sent me to A&E, and there I discovered, to my amazement, that there was something seriously wrong with my heart.

The cardiologist happened to be a regular theatre goer who enjoyed my work. When he took delivery of a new heart-scanning machine, he invited me down to try it out.

The images of my heart had the most incredible clarity. I could see the blood pouring back down into the ventricle from the defective valve. My heart was literally bleeding. And I was seeing an image of my own approaching death.

I thought: *This is the most terrifying thing I have ever seen.* And: *I need never see images of fear or distress in the theatre again.* And: *In my work, I need never create them.* And: *I must try to use my work to heal myself. Perhaps, if I do that, the work will heal others too.*

I was let out the hospital on heavy doses of medication

that alleviated the symptoms whilst I was on the waiting list for surgery.

That summer, I remember going to the Traverse in the festival and standing in the animated crowds in the bar feeling completely alone. There I was, still in mourning for the loss of the love of my life, in the process of changing my gender, waiting for an operation that might end my life... and none of these plays, applauded by critics and audience alike, had anything to say to me at all.

Whatever it was I was going to write, I knew it had to be different.

A month or so later, I was being wheeled to the operating theatre. The surgeon had explained that, in the early stages of the operation, he would have to stop my heart beating. And although he told me the chances of it not starting again were reassuringly low, I knew it was a possibility. And that meant that the eye contact I had with the anaesthetist as they injected me into unconsciousness could be the last human interaction in my life. I tried to accept that. And I tried to make that last moment of consciousness as warm and as loving as I could.

The recovery was very painful, and complicated by my being given an overdose of warfarin soon after the operation. Warfarin was originally developed as a rat poison that kills rodents by thinning their blood. It is useful after heart surgery, but its dosage has to be carefully monitored. I was at home by then and noticed a massive bruise spreading down my arms and all over my chest. I was about to go to bed but thought: If this goes on, I'll die. So I phoned 999 instead.

About two litres of fluid had to be drained from my chest. It was strange to think that the incredible complexity of the surgery I had undergone—where a small plastic ring had been inserted in my heart's mitral valve to repair it—should almost have been undone by a simple lack of communication between my doctor's surgery and the hospital ward.

During these hospital stays, I was registered as a female patient. I was still undergoing the removal of my facial hair;

I think I had the beginning of breasts; and certainly my male genitalia were still unmistakably present. I had to come out again and again in each encounter with medical and nursing staff. And, I guess, in the process, I learnt not to give too much space to shame.

All these experiences helped feed *Queen Jesus* when I eventually found the space to write her in 2008. I'd asked the theatre company to find me a free space in Florence for two–three weeks to write. And they did. And I wrote her very fast, without the time to think about it much, that baking hot summer.

I had been reading the Gospels and trying to think whose story to tell. I had a dear friend at that time who worked as a prostitute off the Royal Mile. Maybe she could be the model for Magdalene. Or maybe it was the story of John. I'd always liked John because we shared the name and because he was the only one without a beard. But when I tried to tune in to these characters, neither of them would speak.

I went to the cathedral on the first day of my stay in Florence, and there was something about the Michelangelo Pieta there that told me it was Jesus. And it became quite easy to tune into him, somehow. I'm not sure why. Perhaps because it did stir a childhood memory of being told that we all have a bit of Jesus inside us, somehow, and that whenever we're in difficulty or trouble we should ask ourselves: *What would Jesus do?* and try to be like him as much as we could.

So that's how the play began. What if Jesus came back to earth here and now? Came back to earth as a trans woman like me. What would she say? What would she do?

So I meditated. And I listened. And the play took shape.

Whenever I adapt a novel, I start with the bits that I love. In that way, the Gospels were no different. There are stories and sayings in the Gospels that move me profoundly. The story of the prodigal son. The story of the woman at the well. The story of the good Samaritan. The story of the woman taken in adultery.

I knew from very early on that my Jesus would not do miracles, because I can't do miracles. And my Jesus would not say anything, or do anything, that I couldn't totally believe and understand myself.

Certainly not just because the traditional church says so.

That meant that my Jesus would not die for our sins, because that belief has never made any sense to me at all; nor would she die and come back to life again, because I find that impossible to believe.

When Susie was dying, I was struck by the immense cruelty of the brain tumour that was killing her. I found myself thinking of how they always used to say that crucifixion was the cruellest death human malice could devise; and how what Susie was going through was a kind of crucifixion, going on for months and months instead of hours and hours...

And then I understood that we all have to go through this. My mother had to. My father had to. My father in law, my mother in law, all those people whose deaths I had witnessed in the hospitals in which I'd worked. All of us.

And then I saw that what the crucifixion meant for me had to do with the need to love each other in the face of death.

The play ended with a communion and a blessing and I finished it in time to catch the flight home.

I sent it to the theatre company in Florence and got no response. I imagine they didn't like it.

I didn't know what to do. But I approached Rachael Rayment, a talented former student who was trying to establish herself as a director, and asked her if she'd direct me. And she did.

And we found a young woman producer who persuaded Glasgay! to commission us for their 2009 Festival and give us £2000. And then she deserted us to become a stand-up comedian and we were on our own.

In the meantime, I had been caught up in the humiliating machinery of trying to obtain surgery to change my gender. The whole process had been interrupted by my heart surgery but had still, somehow, been grinding on. I was obliged to travel down to London to be interviewed by two psychiatrists whose job was to determine whether I fitted the clinical picture of transsexuality, and therefore if I could be referred to a surgeon.

These trips enabled me and Rachael to meet and advance our plans. We were looking for a musician, mainly because I didn't feel able to carry the whole show on my own. We found an amazing percussionist called Adam Clifford.

We decided to limit the seating capacity of the venue to 30; I didn't think I could cope with any more. Colleagues from Queen Margaret University—Sarah Paulley to design the set, George Tarbuck to design the lighting, Morna Baxter to do costume—all got involved.

The names matter. These people gave their skills for very little financial reward. Their generosity made the first production possible.

Together, we were the ones who mainly subsidised the show. Them with their time, and me with my money.

Meantime, the psychiatrists decided that yes, I was clinically trans—as if that was in any way meaningful— and they did refer me to a surgeon, who I scandalised by telling him that no, I did not want the immensely painful and invasive option of gender-reassignment surgery. What I wanted was an end to the hormone war in my body. And an orchidectomy would achieve that.

This is no place to go into graphic details about my genitalia. All you need to know is that the operation is simple, non-invasive, and positively confirmed my identity as a non-binary, third-gender person. And as soon as my body stopped producing male hormones, the insults and abuse in the street came to an end.

Immediately afterwards, I went to France on a writing fellowship, missed a massive furore about the LGBTI art exhibition in Glasgow's modern art gallery, and returned just in time to begin rehearsals in late September.

I was very afraid. It was six years since I had last performed. Since then, I had lost the person I loved most in the world. I had lost my health after heart surgery. I had lost my job in the university. I had lost my male identity. 'John Clifford' had suffered greatly and never really felt at home in the world, but I was at home in his suffering, somehow. 'Ms Jo Clifford' was a step completely into the unknown.

And I was aware that, in writing and performing a serious play about a transgender Jesus, I was doing something no-one had ever done before, or ever imagined doing, and that was emphatically not the kind of thing my colleagues were doing.

I also knew of no other openly trans performers. I felt completely alone.

This sense of vulnerability and isolation deepened when I arrived at the Tron Theatre to prepare for the opening night and found the street full of angry protesters. I had been told that some people were objecting, but the general indifference to what I took to be the much more offensive content of *God's New Frock* had made it hard for me to believe that people would be so angry. And so the scale of the protests very much took me by surprise.

I learnt afterwards that there was a large contingent of Catholics, who had brought a statue of the Virgin Mary, and a large contingent of evangelical Protestants carrying stern placards that read GOD SAYS: MY SON IS NOT A PERVERT and other apparently Christian slogans. Glasgow has a long history of sectarian conflict which tends to deepen the divisions between Protestant and Catholic, but here, the two sides had set aside their hatred for each other and become united in their hatred of me. Eventually, I learned to joke about this and say I was doing my bit for church unity. But on that terrifying evening, jokes were a long way from my mind.

The hatred got worse in the coming days as the tabloid press reported on the demonstration. The BBC had filmed it and posted it on their web site. I gave endless interviews to the papers and broadcast media in the presence of visibly frightened press representatives from the theatre and the Glasgay festival. I remember seeing my picture on the front page of the Glasgow Herald and being frightened in case someone recognised me and beat me up. I remember reading the archbishop's condemnation of me. He said it was "hard to imagine a greater affront to the Christian faith". I felt so distressed. I meant the play to be in praise of Jesus for his humanity and compassion; I couldn't understand why this archbishop would want to condemn it when he hadn't read it and didn't know the first thing about it.

The tabloids made fun of me for being an ex bus conductor, and a trans woman who had written a play that said Jesus was trans. How ridiculous.

I did feel ridiculous. I felt very small and very alone. It was hard to do the play each night, and I remember one performance where I completely forgot to do a whole scene.

All through the week of the run, audience members had to run the gauntlet of protesters. I always crept in via the stage door at the back, which was just as well I suppose. A friend asked a protester why they were so angry about a play they knew nothing about. Wouldn't it be better to see the play before objecting to it?

The protestor replied: "You don't need to go near a sewer to know that it stinks."

Part of me must have believed that to be true, I suppose, because I remember those words but not the lovely words of support and appreciation that other people who sent me, the people who actually saw the show...

A couple of weeks ago, I was talking to a friend who was there who said it was beautiful. She really felt ministered to, she said, she really felt loved. And she also kept looking at the two plain-clothes policemen who were stationed in the theatre to protect me. *What were they thinking?* she wondered. I never noticed them. When I thought about the fact it had been considered necessary to station two police officers in the audience to stop me being physically attacked, I could never make up my mind as to whether this reassured me or terrified me further.

In a culture that habitually regards theatre as irrelevant, and performing a play that in the end simply said we need to love each other, the need for a police presence was just astonishing. What had I done? Why was there so much anger in the air? Why was there so much fear?

After the first night, a gay man was beaten up just outside the theatre. The box-office and Glasgay staff all received threats of violence. I did too; but luckily this was all before Facebook and Twitter were in general use, so very few of the threats and the insults could be directly aimed at me.

When I read all the blogs and all the commentaries, I could pretend this ridiculous trans woman who was apparently saying Jesus was transsexual was maybe someone else. Maybe it was someone else all these people wanted to see dead. Someone else who, all the righteous Christians assured us, was going to suffer so terribly in the deepest pits of Hell. Someone else who was a coward because they hadn't attacked Muhammad. Someone else who was the clearest sign imaginable of the decline and fall of Western civilisation.

But it was me. It was, and as days passed both during and after the run of the play I felt more and more naked, vulnerable and exposed. As if flayed.

I had stopped acting all those years ago because I knew that if I carried on people would come to know that I wanted to be a girl and would hate me. And that I would not survive that hatred. And now it was as if that adolescent nightmare had come true. I *was* acting; people *did* know I wanted to live as a woman; and they *did* hate me.

But I survived.

And I couldn't escape the realisation that somehow I had created something important. The facts spoke for themselves. We had restricted the audience to 30; we had been sold out for all the five nights; and that meant only 150 people had actually seen the show. Yet it had captured the attention of hundreds of thousands more. I felt the show needed to continue. I knew I could not rely on the Scottish theatre industry to do it for me. I knew I had to do it myself. But how?

Both my director and the Glasgay producer made it very clear they wanted nothing more to do with the show. The Scottish theatre critics hadn't reviewed it (they were seeing a show based on the Broons) and none of them had said a word in my defence.

I'd felt my performance had been bad and I didn't see how I could convince anyone otherwise. I felt very traumatised and very alone.

I was rescued by an actor. David Walshe had played She in my *An Apple a Day* earlier that year, and he had seen my *Queen Jesus*. He told me he wanted to work with me as an actor. I was so moved by this.

I said we should probably work with a director. "I know the very one," he said. And that was how I met Susan Worsfold.

I owe so much to her. She's an inspiring and hugely skilled voice teacher as well as a remarkably gifted director. I could not have asked for a better collaborator. She helped me find my voice as a performer and rediscover my joy in performing.

Strangely enough, at first it didn't occur to me to ask her to help with *Queen Jesus*. (We were working with David on a project that eventually became *Sex, Chips and the Holy Ghost* in Glasgow's Oran Mor.)

But working on the project helped my confidence. Performing *Queen Jesus* in my church, Augustine United in Edinburgh, helped so much. A chance came to perform a shortened version in an event called Tranny Hotel in the Adelphi Hotel of Liverpool. That same weekend, I performed to a group of religious professionals based in the city in the Quaker Meeting House.

Chris Goode invited me to perform the show in Exeter's Bike Shed during the preliminary work on his *Albemarle Sketchbook*. I remember going into the theatre space and not having a clue how to perform in it and bursting into tears. But I did perform there and it seemed to work.

When the chance came to perform the show in the Nightingale Theatre, Brighton, as part of the Pink Fringe, I knew I needed help and very nervously asked Susan if she was interested. We split the fee. I remember we bought a sparkly maternity dress from an Oxfam shop and wearing that as my costume. The theatre space was an old hotel dining room, and I remember opening the shutters at one stage to let the light stream in and then banging them shut in another. Susan has a brilliant eye for making the most of unusual spaces and, even though audiences were tiny, it was joy to play to them. We drank champagne in Gatwick airport on the way home.

The next stage was to find a producer. Me and Susan set up various meetings with various established and highly thought of people. But nothing clicked.

Then I got a part in a short film called *High Heels Aren't Compulsory*. The first day of filming was a little difficult because the director had dropped out the night before. The producer was a young queer woman called Annabel Cooper who decided that, in the circumstances, the only thing to do was direct the film herself. She didn't really know what she was doing, as it happened, but the film did get made, and I really liked the way she handled herself in a really difficult situation and asked her if she'd be interested.

She said yes, and we did click. And the adventure began.

For a few years, I'd been trying to find a Fringe venue. The Festival of Justice and Peace at St John's church in Edinburgh's West End seemed like the perfect location. Each year, their artistic director had been enthusiastic, but their acceptance of the show had been knocked back by the festival committee.

2014 was my third attempt. The festival had changed its name to the Just Festival but its stance remained the same. Justice did not extend to a trans performer.

Very much at the last minute, the three of us began looking for another venue. I knew the minister of St Mark's Unitarian Church round the corner. They had a slot free at 10.30pm at night. I'd just sold my house and could invest some of the surplus into the show. And so we performed that fringe!

10.30pm was also the time of the Tattoo fireworks. The venue was very close to the castle, and performing was impossible in the din. The lovely front-of-house man would invite the audience to stand outside, strike up conversation with a stranger, and wait for a lovely surprise.

I'd be sitting up the stairs leading to the church balcony,

waiting for my cue, watching the most incredible light show through the stained-glass window, knowing no-one had ever seen that spectacle before, and no-one would ever see it again.

Audiences were tiny, but among them was Liliane Rebelo, working at that time for the British Council in Brazil. The first of many amazing things she did for us was insist a theatre maker called Natalia Mallo came to see the show. And so I found myself one night shaking hands with this profoundly moved person who was telling me she wanted to translate the show into Portuguese and present it in Brazil and would I let her?

I liked her a lot and said yes, and she sat up all that night to translate it, and we have become such good friends.

And that encounter led us to meet Diego Bagagal the following year when we put the show on in Summerhall, and that led to us performing in a museum in Belo Horizonte, Brazil, in a room full of saints in glass cases. And me collapsing in the middle of the last performance when my heart gave way. And those performances made it possible for Natalia and Gabi and Renata to begin to get bookings for the Brazilian production and for me, later that year, to create a special performance with Uma Só Voz, the choir of homeless people in Rio, for the FLUPP festival in the favela of the City of God.

I loved it there. And in the private houses in Belo Horizonte and São Paulo, in the community centre in Elephant and Castle, the hotel dining room in Brighton, the massive neo-gothic pile in Manchester, the pub basement in Glasgow (where I performed in front of the Rev. Troy Perry, the founder of the Metropolitan Church). I remember the community café in Dumfries, the tiny Unitarian church in Hull. I remember the grandeur of the National Theatre of Uruguay, where I saw Fabiana Fine perform the show in Spanish. I remember the big space in the Traverse, where most of the audience were sitting round a huge long table beautifully decorated with holly and ivy and mistletoe in honour of Christmas.

I remember that on that occasion 26,573 people signed an online petition asking the City of Edinburgh Council to ban the show; and a lonely man with an array of placards that told us THE WAGES OF SIN ARE DEATH keeping a lone vigil outside the Traverse. I remember the bedraggled protestors outside the venue in Belfast, who had brought along a loudhailer, and a man with bagpipes to try to silence my voice.

I remember the man who filmed himself sitting in his car outside St John Chrysostom's Church in Manchester, a bit bewildered because he was the only one trying to protest against me when "the show so clearly breaks the canon law of the Church of England," he said indignantly, holding up his well thumbed leather-bound copy. He'd posted the video on YouTube and the next one to come up was from an evangelical group in America expressing their disgust at the show. "And this" said their commentator, "This is the demon responsible for it." And up came my picture, and I understood that for many people I am evil incarnate.

Which is strange, given that the show celebrates love. I can't begin to understand the reasons for the hatred the show provokes. I worry about the dangers my sisters have faced in Brazil in their courageous resistance to censorship. I love the fact they have taken the show in a completely different direction from ours.

We now have two productions: one for theatrical spaces, and one for everywhere else. We can now perform the show absolutely anywhere.

And I hope we can continue to do so. We have filmed the production, so that people can see it in private in those many countries where it is dangerous to see it in public.

Right now, we are preparing to perform in Brussels; later this year, it will be in Glasgow again, to celebrate the show's tenth anniversary.

I don't know what will happen next. I never have. I never thought the show would last so long, or so many people would see it, or that through it I would come to see myself as a performer.

I'm proud of it. Of all the one hundred plays I have written, perhaps it's this one of which I'm the proudest.

And I think it may be doing some good in the world.

Queen Jesus and Her Bread

For the first years, I couldn't make bread for the show. Performing it scared me too much, and there wasn't really room in my head for anything else.

But when, eventually, I performed the show in St Mark's church for the 2014 Fringe, I incorporated the baking of the bread into the preparations for performance.

The fact I was performing late at night gave me the time to prepare the bread during the day.

The recipe I used—Borodinsky Bread—was an elaborate one involving rye flour and sourdough and malt extract and molasses and coriander seeds that needed to be ground by hand. I got it from a wonderful book called *Bread Matters* by Andrew Whitley (Fourth Estate, 2006) which was in my kitchen at the time of the first production. Rachael Rayment, the show's first director, was staying in my house during rehearsals and, if I remember right, we made it together one special occasion.

It's a complicated bread to make and the effort of getting it right was really helpful in overcoming the nerves of that first run. It tastes incredible, and I loved the expression on the audience's faces when their mouths first savoured it.

The following year in Summerhall, I was performing in the morning and somehow there wasn't time for anything so elaborate. So I made spelt bread instead, which doesn't really need kneading, and still has a very special taste.

It's the best way to prepare for a performance that I know. I loved the feeling of arriving at the performance space with the text in my head and the bread in my hand. Ready with these two gifts to give the audience...

So it was such a joy the following year when the FIT Festival in Belo Horizonte arranged for an oven on the site so I could bake the bread there and give it to the audience still warm from the oven.

I'd recommend everyone learn to bake bread. It gives so much pleasure.

I started with a recipe I got from a book called *Home*

Baked by George and Cecilia Scurfield (Faber, 1956, 1972) and I remember baking bread for everyone in our commune in Merlindene in the mid seventies.

Measurements helped me when I began. This book calls for 2½ pounds flour, ½ an ounce of dried yeast, 2 oz melted butter, ½ an ounce salt and 2 pints warm water. And then you mix it all together and you get a sticky mess.

And then you turn it onto a flour board and then, the book says, "Work through the dough with your fingers and thumbs. Pummel it and punch it and turn it over and over." You add a bit of flour as you go. I'm not so violent: a bit firm and rhythmical and sensuous. And after a bit, a miracle happens. It stops sticking to everything and transforms into "a pleasant, smooth springy dough of a putty like constituency." I love that moment.

I love the next miracle of it rising, of shaping it into a loaf, leaving it rise again, and then baking it in the oven. And what comes out is this delicious, joyful thing you can share with everyone.

In the Bible, Jesus says that the Queendom is like yeast, a tiny quantity of it that an old woman put in a large mass of dough. And by the next morning, the yeast had spread everywhere and the dough was risen (Luke 13:20).

Sometimes I wonder whether Queen Jesus should tell that parable. But perhaps she doesn't need to, because it's in the bread that the audience shares.

The bread she has made with her hands...

The Gospel According to Jesus, Queen of Heaven

by Jo Clifford

The earliest version of *Queen Jesus* was first produced at the Tron Theatre in November 2009 as part of Glasgay!, directed by Rachael Rayment with music by Adam Clifford, lighting design by George Tarbuck, set design by Sarah Paulley and costume design by Morna Baxter.

The next version was first developed at the Pink Fringe in the Nightingale Theatre, Brighton, in 2012, directed by Susan Worsfold.

This current version, printed here, began to take shape at St Mark's Unitarian Church in 2014. It was directed by Susan Worsfold, produced by Annabel Cooper and filmed by Stuart Pratt with stage manager Claire Spiers and costume designer Theo Cleary.

Subsequently, the play has been produced with additional creative support from associate artist Jak Soroka and lighting designer George Tarbuck. Morna Baxter has rejoined the team as costume maker for the current production.

Queen Jesus has been performed many times all over the UK, in all manner of spaces and venues from churches and places of worship (Augustine United in Edinburgh, 2010; St Mark's and Hull Unitarian Churches, 2014 and 2017; and St John Chrysostom's in Manchester with Queer Contact and the Royal Exchange, 2016), to hotel rooms (the Adelphi Hotel in Liverpool, 2011), pubs (Admiral Nelson in Glasgow in the presence of Rev. Troy Perry, founder of Metropolitan Community Church, 2012), community centres (Draper Hall in Elephant and Castle, 2017; The Stove in Dumfries, 2018), universities (Glasgow University Chapel, 2019) and cutting-edge theatres and arts venues (Tron Theatre in Glasgow, 2009 and 2019; Nightingale Theatre in Brighton as part of Pink Fringe, 2012; the Bike Shed in Exeter, 2013; Summerhall in Edinburgh, 2015; The Black Box for Outburst Festival in Belfast, 2015; Traverse Theatre in Edinburgh, 2018).

Internationally, Jo read extracts of *Queen Jesus* in Brno, Ostrava, Wroclaw and Kosice (in the Czech Republic, Slovakia, and Poland) as part of The Authors' Reading Month of 2014. The play was first performed in full out of the UK in Brazil at the FIT-BH international theatre festival in Belo Horizonte in May 2016 and in part later that year in the City of God favela, Rio de Janeiro, as part of FLUPP with Uma So Voz choir of homeless people, and at Theatre de la Vie, for the first Made in Scotland festival in Brussels in June 2019.

The Portuguese translation of the play (translated and directed by Natalia Mallo, with Renata Carvalho in the title role) opened in The International Festival of Londrina (FILO) in October 2016. Since then, it has been performed almost two hundred times in two years, and has attracted huge crowds in every venue. The piece has been performed in every single international festival in Brazil, besides reaching Northern Ireland and being scheduled in Cape Verde and in Portugal. It has been performed in theatres, in cultural centres, and in museums, as well as in homeless shelters, prisons, refuges, churches and even on the streets.

The Spanish translation of the play (also translated and directed by Natalia Mallo, with Fabiana Fine in the title role) opened in the Teatro Solis in Montevideo, Uruguay, in October 2017 with Fabiana Fine in the title role before moving to the Festival International de Buenos Aires (FIBA) in the same month.

ENTER JESUS WITH A CASE. EVERYTHING SHE NEEDS FOR
THE SHOW IS CONTAINED WITHIN IT. SHE UNPACKS AS
SHE SPEAKS:

This is the time
This is the place
This is where we meet each other

And you may think
because I'm Jesus
we should meet in a church
But, I tell you, so many churches hate me
hate me and fear me
because I somehow seem to threaten who they are
People too. People in the street
shout at me because I threaten who they are

You must be very brave to have me here

But then, we never met in churches anyway
Not when I lived as a man
all those centuries ago

We used to meet in people's rooms
and we'd always know where to go
because a queer person would guide us there

They suppressed a lot in my story
but this was something they could not altogether hide
You'll find it in Mark. And Luke
Dear Mark. Dear Luke

And we know the person was queer because
the stories say we had to look
for a man carrying a water pitcher
And men don't do that
It's women's work
Men are too ashamed

1

It's a strange thing in this world
that men are proud to carry guns and knives
proud to carry the instruments of death
but ashamed to carry the source of life

But she wasn't ashamed
the dear soul who guided us
She was beautiful
this person born male
wearing a woman's dress
and with jasmine in her hair
guiding us here

She was one of us

And this is how it all began. A group of us,
meeting as friends
because we wanted to change the world

I don't know why they started saying we were only twelve
I mean there were sometimes less, but mostly more
Or why they said we were only men
Some of us are men:
Dear Matthew, the tax collector
who, like us, was an outcast
and Philip, who baptised the eunuch
and John, who I so truly love

But there are women too
of course there are
Wild women, free women:
Mary, Martha and Salome

So yes, some of us are men and some of us are women
and some of us are men who used to be women
and some of us are women who used to be men
and some of us are both at once

and we confuse people
and I love that in us most of all

Because we are the hijra from India
and the kathoey from Thailand
and the waria from Indonesia
and the bissu from the Archipelago
and the fa'fa'fine from Samoa
and the muxe from Mexico
and the travesti from Brasil
and the two-spirit people from North America
and the shamans from Siberia
and the yan daudu from Nigeria
and many more besides

And verily, verily I say unto you
because it is undoubtedly true
that every culture
in every place and time
has known of us, and celebrated us
mostly
except for this one
and it is in the minority

And I don't understand why now
in those few places on this tormented earth
where we openly flaunt our dear and beautiful selves
we should so often have to live off the streets
as harlots and whores

But I honour us anyway
all of us
For to be us, to embody this so-called shame
and this disgrace
is a privilege
and it is an honour
for the last shall be first
and the first last

3

And remember, all of you:

I never said: Beware the homosexual
and the transgendered
and the queer
because our lives are unnatural
or because we are depraved in our desires

I never said that

I said: Beware the self-righteous and the hypocritical
Beware those who imagine themselves virtuous
and pass judgement,
those who condemn others
and think themselves good

Their lips are full of goodness
but their hearts full of hatred

and that is why I said: Woe unto you
scribes and hypocrites!
whited sepulchres!
that on the outside look so sleek and smooth
but on the inside are a mass of filth and corruption!

And that is why I said: Beware of them
and never never never beware the homosexual
and the transgendered
and the queer!

Because I, Jesus of Nazareth
was and am one of them
I always was queer
I always am queer
and I always shall be queer
from now until the end of time!

And that's the sermon over

Sermons can be so difficult!
But look at you
You've just listened to one
Very beautifully
How clever are you

And my plan isn't to preach sermons
My plan is to tell stories
Me and my poor tired body
that every day gets closer to death

Shall we start at the beginning
you and me and Saint George of the lights?
Start at the beginning of everything
at the time of the great darkness

THE LIGHTS GO OUT

And behold,
there is darkness
darkness upon the face of the deep

And my mum saw the dark
and said: *Let there be light*
And look, there is light

And wasn't she clever?
And isn't it beautiful?
Shall we do it again?
Look. Look
So lovely

I love my mum
and I am the daughter of God
and almost certainly the son also

My mum said: *Let there be light*
And I say: *I am the light*
And I am

And that's why I'm here:
to bring the light
bring the light to a dark place

And that's why you're here also
to bring light to dark places

Because when my mum made the great big light in the sky
she took a little bit of that light

and put it inside each one of us
and it is still there
however much darkness we may feel there is inside us
and however much darkness there may be in our world
there is still a light. There is still a light inside us

There's a light inside each one of us
and our job is to let it out to shine

> THE SPACE IS GRADUALLY BEING LIT AGAIN, BY JESUS AND
> THE AUDIENCE, ONE CANDLE AT A TIME

And look
that's just what you're doing
you clever things

's why an angel came to your mum
.....ounce your birth
And she did come, the angel, and she did say:
Blessed art thou among women
said it to your mum

Did your mum never tell you that?

No? That's strange
It must have a been a big thing for her
It was a big thing for mine
She wrote a song about it and everything

Maybe your mum heard the angel and forgot
Maybe she was doing the ironing at the time,
or driving to work
or filling in a tax return

Tax returns are so complicated
They don't leave space for angels

And you can't blame her, because we all do it
We almost always do forget

and so the angel goes away weeping

But you, and you, and you, and me:
we still grew in our mummy's tummies
The miracle still occurred,
and we somehow came into the world

And our conception was immaculate
because it happened through sex
and sex in itself is innocent and is pure

I know my mum and dad made love to each other
and I don't know if they did it in the missionary position
or whether she was on top

or whether they did it like dogs
But they did it towards the end of March
when winter was over, and just at the beginning of spring

Now I don't know if they enjoyed it
—my mum never said—
But I hope they did
I hope they had pleasure
because pleasure is sacred
pleasure is holy

and that's one reason why
ever so much later on
why, much later on, I invented communion:
so we could eat together
and offer each other our bodies, saying
        This is my body
and drink together
        This is my blood
and then have pleasure
for what should feel like the end of time
and give thanks
        Thank you, my darling
        Thank you, my love
and go home rejoicing

just like the shepherds did in the story of our birth
Do you remember them?
The ones who were tending their flocks by night

And the angels were saying:
        Fear not.
        I bring you tidings of great joy
        You shall find the babe lying in a manger.

And that was you, and you, and you
and me too. All of us
in our swaddling clothes

dear little things that we were
and still are

And don't you go telling me
there weren't any shepherds
or that there weren't any flocks
because they all went years ago
when they built the city by-pass

or that it wasn't a manger
but a plastic box
in a run-down maternity ward

or there were no wise men
maybe just your dad
and him a bit pissed maybe
being so nervous

Think poetically

because what I tell you is true
the whole truth and nothing but

because, beloved sisters and brothers
and every kind of sibling in Christ

because I am the truth
and I am also the way and the life
and a million other lovely things besides

and the angels were there at your birth
and there was rejoicing and great gladness
and wise men did come with the most beautiful gifts
and the angels, just so delightfully framing the sky
and all to announce the birth of a baby

The other week my daughter said:
Dad, you're going to be a grandma

and how happy we all were

Maybe we love babies because they know
just what they're doing

That's why I told everybody to be like a little child
and said that was the way to enter the queendom of heaven
That's why I told everybody, starting with myself

because by the time we've grown up and become adults
the world has messed us up
mostly
and we blunder about

SHE LIGHTS A CANDLE

There was a man came to me once
and said: *Mistress, how should I live?*

And I said: *How do you think?*

And he said: *Well, I suppose, they told me once at school...*

What did they tell you once at school?

    To love your neighbour

You do that then

    But what if I can't stand the sight of him?
    And who is my neighbour anyway?

There was a man once, on his way home
from the centre of town to Leith
and it can be rough down Leith Walk late at night
and he got mugged and beaten and left for dead

And a bishop came by
on his way home from a synod
and synods are places where lots of older men get bad
    tempered about sex
and his heart was weary with dissension and hatred
And he saw the needy man and thought:
    It's probably a junkie.
    Brought it on himself.
    I'll pray for him when I get home
And so he drove on

And a policeman went past
on his way home at the end of his shift
And he was tired and weary
of the spectacle of human suffering
And he thought: *Just another junkie.*
    There's nothing I can do.

I'll pray for him when I get home
And so he drove on

And then a queen came past
staggering a little because she'd been to Sofi's Bar and got
    herself drunk as a skunk
and bust her heel on the way home
and her dress was torn
and her make-up was smudged
and her stockings were all ladders
and there was the taste of cum on her lips
and she saw the man and she thought: *Poor sod*
and she phoned an ambulance on her mobile
and then she stayed with him till the ambulance came

And which of those was his neighbour?

And is it really that complicated?

SHE LIGHTS A CANDLE

I was at a standpipe once during a water shortage
and I met a woman there
The dear love was exhausted
because she'd been queuing for hours
and she had that battered look that women have when
     they've been battling hostility and rejection all their lives
She was black, maybe, in an area where people were meant
     to be white
or maybe the other way round

or maybe she was simply a woman
That is enough to make you an outcast
in so many places in this terrible world

She was standing in line with her container
and I had none

And she said: *Without a container they will not let you drink*
because the water was strictly rationed

And I said: *Someone will give me drink*

And she said: *They will not*
          because everyone is so thirsty

And there was something in the way she looked at me
so I understood something about myself

because I said: *Like you, they will drink of this water*
          and then will be thirsty again
          But me, I have a kind of water inside me
          that will never dry up
          It's like a kind of bubbling spring deep,
          deep inside the soul of me
          welling up sweet, cool water for ever
          and those who drink it need never be afraid of death

And I could tell she believed me

so I looked at her
and I saw
and I said: *You have that water inside you too*

And in a moment
another moment
she'd have been free...

But then something happened
and the crowd got difficult
and I lost that poor woman
I lost her for ever
for the crowd had swallowed her up
and she was gone

And that's how it is

When you lose an earring
you don't care about the one you still have
marooned and useless on the bathroom shelf
It's the one you lost that you care about

It's the same when you lose one of your kids in the
    supermarket
That's the one you care about, not the whining brats
    tugging at your skirts

There was once a father who had two sons

And the younger son came to know she was his daughter
and didn't know what to do
In the end, she went to her father saying: *Forgive me,*
        for I can no longer be called your son

But the father did not forgive her,
but called the whole household together and said:
        This creature has brought disgrace on all of us
and he cast her out

But the poor man was only doing what he thought he
    should
and, in spite of everything, he still loved his child
so he slipped her a load of money on the side

And the daughter who had once been a son went off to a far
    country, and then
—not being very inclined to be prudent—
spent all the money her father had given her
on gorgeous dresses and shoes
and soon found herself out on the street without a euro to
    her name
and all her friends
—who loved her when she wore Prada and Versace—
now called her a chav
and would have nothing to do with her

And there she was
in a far country where there was no-one to help her
And what was she to do?
Well, she had to take work where she could find it
so she worked in a hotel kitchen
cleaning pots and pans

And it was dirty work
and the hours were long

and the pay was wretched
and she often went hungry
and in the kitchen they threw out much food
that in her father's house would have made very good food
   for the pigs
but they had to throw it away
for they were not allowed to touch it

And she said to herself: *In my father's house*
     they treat the animals better
     than they treat the workers in this place
     I will go back to my father and say
     I am so, so sorry, but I cannot be your son
     and if you cannot accept me as your daughter
     then at least employ me as your cleaning maid

So she went back to her father's house
hitching rides and hiding in goods wagons

And her father saw her coming from a long way off
and shouted out for joy and ran out to meet her

And she fell at his feet and said, *Father*
but the father would not let her finish

He helped her onto her feet
and he embraced her
and said to his household: *Run her a scented bath*
     and fetch her a gorgeous dress
     and crack open the best champagne
     and let's have a party!
     For she that was gone has returned
     and she that was dead has come back to life
     and she that was lost has been found

And when the party was in full swing
the elder son came home from the office
And he asked, *What is this?*

for their house tended to be a very serious kind of place

And when he heard, he was furious
and he said to his father: *I have been such a good son!*
I have done everything I was supposed to
and you haven't so much as bought me a decent suit!
But when this pervert comes home
it gets everything!

And the father said: *It's true you've always done your best*
and tried to be a good son to me
but the fact is you're rather dull
and you have never loved me!
And you have lost yourself...

...whereas this new daughter of mine was dead
and is now alive
She was lost
and is now found
I have found her
and she has found herself

And so of course we must celebrate.

And so they did

Because the queendom is like that
The queendom is like a grain of mustard seed
        tiny tiny tiny
and you can try to hide it if you like
but, if you do, it will grow inside you
        big big big
until it feels like there is no room for anything beside it

For, I tell you, that which was hid shall come to light
for inside us we all have a light
and it's maybe the very thing that we have been taught to
    be most ashamed of

And when you have a light, do you hide it in a closet?
No! You bring it out into the open where everyone can see it
and be glad it exists to shine in the world

SHE LIGHTS A CANDLE

They might try to put out your light
They might hate you for allowing it to shine
They might spit on you or shout after you
        Faggot! Pervert! Maricón!
or maybe they'll shout
        Look! It's a geezer!
or call you a pervert or an open sewer
They might do worse: they might
beat you
or torture you
and kill you
and throw your body into a skip

because these things happen

But I say to you:
Bless you if people abuse you or persecute you
for being who you are
because it means you are bringing about change

And bless those who persecute you too
because hatred is the only talent that they have
and it really doesn't amount to much

They will lose it in the end
for no matter what they say or do
change is coming

and, one day, the world will be free

SHE LIGHTS A CANDLE

And why do we resist?
Why can't we celebrate?

There was a wedding once

We were invited and they run out of wine
and they all turned to me to ask me what to do
so I handed out water
water in flagons
and I said: *Drink this*
        It will be as good as wine

And it was...

And then the dancing started
and as we dance, we take our pleasure
pleasure in the intellect
in the elegant architecture of the dance
in the pleasing coordination of the feet
pleasure in the graceful movement of the arms
pleasure in the belly, in the sacrum and the sacred groin
in the fine downy hair growing up our companion's legs
in the bristly hair growing down their chin
in the gorgeous curly hairs on their testicles
the playful little ones round their vagina

        a hand's caress
        on the arms
        the legs
        the buttocks
        and those oh-so-sensitive places between the thighs

pleasure in giving, pleasure in receiving
pleasure in feeling
pleasure in pleasure

Life, life coming
life coming to give life

Our Mother, who art on Earth
blessed is your name
Your joy be here on Earth
as it is in Heaven
Give us this day our daily kisses
Forgive us our stupidity
as we forgive those stupidities done to us
Lead us not into self-righteousness or rage
and save us from destruction and negativity
For thine is the Queendom
the beauty and the joy
for ever and ever. Amen

There was a woman that I met once
who had given herself to life and to loving
and so of course they wanted to kill her

They thought they had caught her in adultery
the church men, the scribes and the pharisees
They arrested and held her and condemned her to death

and they said to me: *Can this wicked woman live?*
hoping to trap me, somehow,
so they would have an excuse to kill me too

I can see her standing there, in the centre of the circle
She doesn't look away
She doesn't ask for mercy or for pity
She stands there and she looks her judges in the eye

They give me a stone
Kill her, they said
It is our law

And I look at the woman
and I look at the stone
and I hold the stone here in my hand

How beautiful a thing
how full of slow patient life
How can I use it to give death?
What kind of crime is that?

Far, far worse than anything this woman is meant to have
    done
She's probably just run away from an abusive husband
or maybe she has suffered rape
for these things happen

But supposing she has done something bad
suppose she has stolen

suppose she has killed someone
suppose she has stood by and let
her child be trafficked or raped
Am I still better than her?
Are you? Are you? Are you?

There is a bruise on her face
just beside her right eye
I reach out as if to touch it
and I know

I know we all stumble over our mother earth
all of us stumbling together
We have no right or business to condemn
so I look at the ground and I say:
> Let the one who is without fault
> be the first to throw a stone

And I listen as one by one
the stones all fall to the ground

And in the end they're gone
only I and the woman remain
and I say to her: *Let's go. Let's go and try to sin no more*

And I'm out in the street
and I'm battered by the traffic
with that woman's look of gratitude
as if branded on my soul

What has she got to be grateful for?
All I did was treat her like a human being
Has no-one ever done that to her before?

All the faces
all the faces passing
with their tales of dreadful suffering to tell

This is where we get crucified:
>   in the street
>   in the office
>   in the job we detest that uses about *this* much of our
>   creativity or our talent
>   in the job that demands we cheat and we exploit and
>   we grind down our fellow human beings
>   in the job we don't have and so we're made to feel like
>   shit because we're jobless
>   with the partner who oppresses and cheats us
>   or who we don't love any more
>   in the lonely room where there's no-one to care for us
>   or where there's no-one for us to love

This is where it happens
This is the place of the skull
This is the place of darkness
This is where we get crucified

I can hear them sawing the planks to make the crossbars
and driving in the nails. I feel them
I feel them going in to my feet and hands

But don't imagine I'm the only one
Don't imagine it's only going to happen to me
and that I'll do it to expiate your sins

I can't do that:
your sins are your sins, mine are mine
and we will all hang on our cross

And that cross will be a hospital bed, maybe
>   a road-traffic accident
>   cancer
>   or even maybe a bomb
>   heart failure
>   stroke, brain tumour
>   or a birth that goes most terribly wrong

And it will torment us,
sometimes slowly, sometimes fast

Let's pray it happens fast
and the torment is gentle
and the passing is swift

But, quick or slow, gentle or harsh
it will torment us
torment us till we have to let go of living

That's the price we pay for being born

I see that, and I know that
and that's why I call my friends together—
all my friends
all my family
all my lovers
—so we can eat and drink together
And why this happens each day, each hour
in my name, some place on this tormented earth

That is why I take the bread and I break it

ALL THE CANDLES ON THE ALTAR ARE LIT.

AS SHE SPEAKS THESE WORDS, SHE BREAKS THE BREAD,
SHE POURS THE WINE

This is my body
Like yours, it will be broken
Eat this
Remember me

And why I pour the wine
Drink this
Remember me
This is my blood
Like yours, it will be shed

This is our body that will be broken
This is our blood that will be shed

All of us in this together
All of us here to love and to be loved

Remember. Remember. Remember

EVERYONE HAS SHARED BREAD AND WINE.

SHE INVITES THEM TO STAND. SHE INVITES THEM TO
HOLD HANDS. SHE BLESSES THEM:

Bless the timid and the shy
for we shall be shameless

Bless the lonely and misunderstood
for we shall have everyone we want

Bless the poor
for we shall be rich

Bless the chairman of the board
for we shall certainly lose everything!

Bless the boy in the closet in the silk wedding gown
for we shall come out

Bless the prostitute
for we shall be honoured

Bless the frigid and the impotent
for we shall have sex for ever and ever!

Amen! Amen!

And bless the fathers who don't care because they've never
    been cared for
For we shall be loved

Bless the mothers who hit because they cannot still their
    children's tears
for we shall be comforted

Bless the bully and the criminal
for we shall lose all fear

Bless the sad and fearful souls who go into government
for we shall one day learn to do good in the world

Bless the people who bomb and who shell and who starve
    other people they take to be their enemies
and bless the enemies who fight back as best they can
for they shall all come to know they are one people in the
    end

Amen! Amen!

And bless all of us in this beautiful city
Bless us in our times of joy and happiness
and in all the times we have been frozen in terror

Remind us we are not alone
Don't let us ever forget
for he is she
and she is he
and we are they
and they are we
and ever shall be
for ever and for ever and for ever

Amen!

This is the time
This is the place

This is the time to say: Goodbye

Testimonies

from those involved in the *Queen Jesus* story

The Original Production

Queen Jesus was first performed in November 2009 at the Tron Theatre in Glasgow as part of the annual Glasgay! Festival. The mostly self-funded production was assembled on a modest budget, but its impact was huge. As news of the play spread and high-profile commentators spoke out to condemn it in the tabloid press, hundreds of protestors gathered outside the theatre and a half a million online protests appeared on blogs and social media platforms. All through the week-long run, audience members had to run a gauntlet of protesters

Rachael Rayment

Director of the original production

I had known Jo since 2001, when she was a professor at Queen Margaret University and my thesis supervisor. Back then, I knew her as John Clifford. I moved to America to study dramaturgy at the American Repertory Theatre Institute, and we stayed in touch as John's life underwent profound changes in the intervening years. When I moved back to the UK in 2008 and first encountered *Queen Jesus*, John was now Jo.

The exact flow of events that led to me directing Jo in her play are slightly fuzzy in my memory now. I remember her sending me some of her most recent work, reading *Queen Jesus* and asking if I could direct a production. It would be my first professional directing gig in the UK. And something of a trial by fire...

I was drawn to the play because it was so profoundly personal and intimate. For me, the play was about Jo, her Christian faith, her relationship to Jesus, the teachings of the Gospels and a defiant public expression of self. The very act of performing it was, as Jo herself says, a confrontation and exorcism of shame. At its core, it touched upon a deep sense of sacredness, humanity and compassion that was universal. I didn't have to be trans, or Christian, to understand and be deeply moved by it.

I knew the play had political resonance, but felt it would be more powerful if I focused on the personal and the sacred. I felt the political was obvious enough without needing any directorial highlighting. My aim was to showcase Jo in her professional debut as a trans performer, and make sure that she had what she needed to feel confident and supported on stage. As a director, it was an opportunity to play with blurring the lines between religious, sacred ritual and theatrical performance—one grew directly out of the other, after all. This even extended to Jo and I starting every rehearsal with 15 minutes of meditation together.

When you make a piece of art and release it into the public arena, as is often said, it stops being yours. Once our production left the confines of the rehearsal room, it hit the media headlines and sparked a maelstrom of debate, excitement and outrage. I remember watching it all happen, like a movie playing on loop, feeling oddly disassociated from it. The reaction felt so far removed from what we had done during rehearsals. And I remember wishing that all of the protestors would come and see the play, as I was convinced that many of them would be surprised when they realised it wasn't what they expected. A bit naive of me, perhaps! But I do wonder how many would have had their preconceptions shattered if they had just watched the show.

In any case, I am so happy that we did it and that I was there with Jo for the first performance. And I am so glad that it's still going ten years later.

George Tarbuck

Lighting designer on the original production in 2009. George returned to light the show in 2018 for the Christmas run at the Traverse Theatre

I first worked with Jo when I lit her play *Losing Venice* at the Traverse Theatre in 1985. I went on to light several of Jo's other productions, including *Playing with Fire*, *Ines de Castro*, *Light in the Village*, and *Lucy's Play*.

There is a strong thread running through Jo's work of being on the side of the marginalised, powerless and dispossessed. There is a feeling throughout the work that there might be a better way to live.

The lighting for the original *Losing Venice* was done in open white light; the subtleties in the lighting came from playing with levels, taking the piece from candlelight to blinding sunlight. *Queen Jesus* is also lit in open white light. There is an honesty and inclusiveness about white light, it contains every colour but is more than the sum of them.

Queen Jesus is an important play for troubled times. It is a meditation on acceptance and love; it is a light in a dark place.

Marco Biagi

A former SNP MSP and equalities minister. Marco saw the first production of Queen Jesus at the Tron

I love theatre, but, like exercising, I don't do it often enough. Yet, once in a while, a description leaps off the page. So it was for *Queen Jesus*.

Having once been in a Fringe production of Terrence McNally's *Corpus Christi*—aka the gay Jesus play—I instantly wanted to see this new kid on the block. A gay Messiah was too much for some people, but a trans one? They wouldn't stand for it on the letters pages! (Post-millennials, those are what angry people had before Twitter.)

Indeed, shuffling into the Tron on a dark Scottish November evening, the placard-waving of the protestors outside seemed like the first act, outraged as they denounced a blasphemy they deemed abhorrent.

I did wonder how many theatregoers came wanting blasphemy—*Jerry Springer: The Opera* with a Glaswegian accent or some schlocky horror show. Instead, we were offered a work that was intimate, authentic and personal: a communion, in the truest sense of the word; a meditation, on the importance of love and acceptance; and, indeed, a lamentation that could not but be imbued with the author's own ongoing lived experience. Sadly, for some that is blasphemy; for me it is true veneration.

In the years since, I have often had need amidst chaos to recall the unbowed piety of *Queen Jesus*. Too often, in fact. She was a study in poise, an amazing grace that stands out in a world turned to rage—and a rage so often directed at people like her. She must have needed to call upon it far more than I.

Yet, a decade on, I cannot but be reassured and filled with rediscovered hope every time I hear that she is preaching her Gospel again—and that she has new audiences, all eager to hear it.

Andy Arnold

Artistic director at the Tron since 2008. Andy programmed the original production of Queen Jesus in 2009, and the tenth anniversary production for 2019

It's truly wonderful when theatre has a real impact on people's lives and stirs the emotions—that's what we all strive for when making it. Well, the impact of the opening performance of *Queen Jesus* ten years ago at the Tron was monumental. At least three hundred people shouted and complained outside the building against what they believed to be sheer and utter blasphemy. Of course none of these protesters had actually seen the show—that might have undermined their prejudices against it.

I'm thrilled that this groundbreaking show by Jo is returning to the Tron ten years later.

UK Productions

Since its explosive premiere in 2009, Queen Jesus has been performed many times all over the UK in all manner of spaces and venues, from churches and places of worship to pubs and community centres, hotel rooms, and cutting-edge arts venues.

Susan Worsfold

Director, designer and founding director of Queen Jesus Productions

Queen Jesus is a work of devotion. Of devotion to ourselves and to being present with one another. To commune. It is constantly evolving, changing and deepening, dependant on where those of us who create it are in ourselves and where the audience are in their lives. To witness this is an ongoing journey and a continuous barometer of where the personal present meets the politics of its time.

Jo and I met directly after the first production of *Queen Jesus* at the Tron in 2009. I will be forever grateful to the extraordinary actor and dear friend, David Walshe, who introduced us. He had seen the original performance and knew he wanted to perform with Jo, to be close to her compassion. I led a voice workshop with Jo and David, bringing us together through the Nadine George Voice Work (NGVW).

Jo's connection with the work was immediate, and the trauma that she had experienced through the violent reception of that first *Queen Jesus* rose to the surface. Isolation, vulnerability, hurt and distress were all present, as well as a fierce determination to not be silenced.

I have been working with NGVW since 1994 and it is a core part of my own directing practice. At its heart, this voice work offers space for acceptance—of an embodied breath and the radical implications of taking space, of an expansion in our voice and therefore in our own identity, of an invitation to be more of ourselves not more than ourselves, of the male and female mix of energies that lie in us all, of letting go of personality layers and shedding defensive skin to sit with our own essence. It is these guiding principles that informed Jo and I's initial journey.

It led us to create, with David, a new commission for Òran Mór's A Play, A Pie and A Pint series, *Sex, Chips and The Holy Ghost*. In it, a transexual nun and a gay priest get excommunicated from the Catholic church and set up a dowsing business called Soul Clean Dot Com. And this in turn led to a Channel 4 commission to create a short script and film with these infectiously joyful, courageous and careering crusaders.

It was from this place of creative connection that Jo and I entered into the touring production of *Queen Jesus*. We faced the text to see where it now resonated with Jo. I always saw this work as a barometer piece for Jo—for her to see where she is in herself each time the evolution of performing it presents itself. In identifying this for Jo, I was identifying it in myself also. We started gently, stripping back the framing elements of the text to crystallise the chapters.

It was completely organic to respond to the environment in our first carefully considered outing to the Pink Fringe at the Nightingale Theatre, Brighton (2012). Steven Brett, the artistic director at this time, beautifully held a space for us to explore a short edited version where we promenaded the audience around the backstage of the theatre, opening the shutters to let the light into the black-box space and asked the audience to see one another as we sat in a circle and shared communion. It was here that our world with Jesus in its new form began to clarify: to be boutique, bespoke, site-specific and site-responsive work. We intentionally developed and designed *Queen Jesus* to enable us to travel as lightly and as far afield as possible.

And in those first years, Jo and I quietly built our work and our practice, holding space for one another, training, learning and deepening our understanding of the text, of ourselves and of our presence. This text has given form and distance to the layers of oppression and pain that Jo experienced in her life, and our practice together enabled that initial hurt to transform itself. It was an intimate school of theatre, at times intense, quietly confronting but always fulfilling.

Meeting Annabel Cooper, our co-founding director and producer, felt like coming home to family. Each of us has learnt with one another along the way in relation to creating work and to building our company, Queen Jesus Productions. And each of us has grown, expanded and shed skin. It has not always been an easy path. As discoveries are made and honesties found, the body responds and there have been many life and health journeys for each of us to support.

Expanding this family to connect with our Brazilian sisters Natalia Mallo, Renata Carvalho and producer Gabi Gonçalves has been an artistically and humanly humbling journey.

Natalia translated the text almost overnight. It has been extraordinary to witness her, Gabi and Renata's artistry, ability and embodied creative power in building the Brazilian production to where it is truly breaking new ground today. Renata's performance is spellbinding. Their transformation through the journey of *Queen Jesus* confirms the strength of a work which can hold space for all cultures and interpretations. And to meet sisters who work with such fierce devotion is joyous and at times overwhelming.

Our own journeys to Brazil and the sisters who have enabled this to happen—Liliane Rebelo, Paulo Souza Lopez, Julianete Azevedo—deepened our world. A specific thanks is given to the inspiring artist Diego Bagagal who initially invited us to the International Theatre Festival in Belo Horizonte, Brazil in 2016. Each of these creative practitioners work with compassion and courage that has guided our own growth here in the UK.

The Gospel According to Jesus, Queen of Heaven reflects the desire to understand where Jesus would travel to today and who she would commune with. For Queen Jesus Productions, we want to respond to all spaces and invitations and the most important resource for us is time. To reside in the space in which we are presenting, to connect to its community and atmosphere and so to see where the roots of the message resonate with where we find ourselves. And in doing so, we hopefully deepen the connection and the intimacy of the work. This has taken us to museums, safe-space cafés, hotel rooms and churches amongst many other places, and in each place and space it is a new production, a new staging, a new work.

In our new production at the Traverse in December 2018, we came full circle. We created a new model for the play, responding to the main-stage space of Traverse 1. It's core staging element is a banquet size table, measuring the width of the audience seating bank, with the audience choosing onstage/table or auditorium seating. The length of this table is the anchor between all main stage spaces we tour to, responding in size to the width of each theatre's auditorium seating. We are now mixing both our boutique and main-stage elements and approaches.

The audience has grown, not only in numbers but in diversity. We now have invitations from a variety of religious groups, academic departments, LGBTQIA+ communities as well as traditional theatre spaces and arts festivals. The invitations range from private performances for curated communities to using the production as an educational tool in religious and theatrical studies and in training days, as well as being published in academic journals. *Queen Jesus* has grown in recognition as an intersectional piece of many themes that are evolving in current public discussion.

We have grown. Writer has become performer, director to designer, producer to production designer and performer. Jo and I have continued our creative collaborations together into *Eve* for the National Theatre of Scotland and *War in America* for the Attic Collective at Edinburgh Festival Theatres, amongst others.

We have built our own model of creating theatre, crafting presence. We have made conscious and unconscious decisions to take the steps we needed to take, work in the way we needed to work, to have the creative, confronting and courageous conversations we've needed to have. Evolving through one text, one frame, over ten years has enabled a deepening of our practice, message and friendship. A move against conventional timeframes of creation. A commitment to being in a relationship which deepens an understanding of self, edging towards a possibility of transcending your own ego.

We don't bring a play, we bring a world. How we are with one another, how we consider one another, how we love one another directly impacts on how we open the doors to ourselves and to the audience.

This is always the time. This is always the place. This is always where we meet each other.

Annabel Cooper

Producer and founding director of Queen Jesus Productions

I first encountered *Queen Jesus* in a seedy bar in Edinburgh in 2013. We had just launched Dive—a new queer club night "for, by and of the people." I'd heard about Jo and her trans Jesus and seen the iconic image of her with the stigmata. Needless to say Jo wasn't your typical club performer and she was way out of our league, but as she was such a pillar of the queer community I asked her to perform anyway. We had no money and nothing of a reputation back then but miraculously—the first of many miracles—she agreed to perform in early August 2013 and bless the start of the Fringe. Jo walked into our fabulously dingy cabaret venue among the drag queens, kings and club kids and brought an equanimity and power that shone through the frenetic Fringe energy, catching on the mirrorball and shimmering over glitter. Seeing her perform the text for the first time and offer this beautiful gift to our little, unknown, club night was very moving. I understood for the first time that *Queen Jesus* belongs everywhere. She's just as at home in clubs, pubs, community centres, queer spaces and dive bars as she is in churches and fancy theatres. She's wherever she needs to be and whoever she needs to be present with. And at that moment, we needed her in our fledgling little queer space among our newly found queer family.

Jo and I have worked together ever since and she and Queen Jesus would perform many more times at Dive as our night grew into a company of artists that would celebrate many successful Fringe runs. Jo had seen something in me that we shared, and although I didn't realise it at the time this bond would help me develop an understanding of myself and a practice rooted in resistance and my queerness. After collaborating on a short film together (*High Heels Aren't Compulsory*) Jo emailed to say she and the director of *Queen Jesus* were having problems finding a venue for their self-funded Fringe run in 2014. St John's had pulled out at the last minute and they needed a producer. I didn't have any experience putting on plays, but as soon as I met Susan and Jo there was no doubt in my mind that I would take the job. I'm very grateful for the trust and faith they showed in me and everything I've learnt from them. I could never have predicted where our partnership has taken us—geographically, creatively and spiritually, together and personally. *Queen Jesus* is a lifelong commitment and Jo and Susan are my family. We've travelled the world together, overcome challenges and shared life-altering experiences and as we travel through time and space our family grows and changes everyone it encounters. It would have been impossible to imagine the enormity of what would unfold and everything our incredible sisters in Brazil have gone through, but I know we'll be together for whatever comes next.

Although she's performed all over the world in beautiful theatres and prestigious festivals, I'll always cherish my first encounter with *Queen Jesus*. Back in that dive bar, speaking directly to the outsiders that needed to hear her most, sharing joy, celebration and resistance, in a space carved out, for a short time, only for us.

Miriam Attwood

Founder and director of StorytellingPR. Miriam and her team have helped Jo, Susan and Annabel communicate with the media since 2015.

I first encountered *Queen Jesus* when I was approached to work on it. Knowing Jo's work, I didn't hesitate to say yes. What I found, as a Church of England-raised LGBTQ+ ally and creative, was a soothing and magical way to process my experiences of the church that I had found uncompromising.

Possibly the easiest way for me to express how I feel about *Queen Jesus*, is to share here how I talk about the show. Which goes a little something like this:

"Do you know Jo Clifford? Well if not you should. She's quite incredible, and she has created this space which is so comforting, so full of all of the messages of warmth and love and joy and inclusion that are in the New Testament, but she has inverted the pronouns and made it real. I am someone who knows the Anglican order of service off by heart (repeated drills as a child!) and a politically-minded tub-thumping feminist. She gave me back access to that gentle world—the care for the weak, the alone, the marginalised—by a simple and incredibly genuine rereading and rewriting of what has far to often become a textbook for hate and misunderstanding, but never really was. Jo, and Queen Jesus, give us back our love in a ceremony to be celebrated."

Chris Goode

Artistic director of Chris Goode & Company

The first time I saw *Queen Jesus*, live and in the flesh, was in 2013. Jo had come to be part of a mini-season I'd programmed at a now-closed (and much-missed) little indie theatre in Exeter. I didn't know her too well back then, but we were proud to have her with us, and thrilled to be bringing Jesus to town. On arriving at the venue, Jo looked around at that characteristically fringey performance space—quirky, admittedly; a bit damp, perhaps—and burst into tears. I was horrified! What had I done? This was evidently not what Jo had been expecting.

How we got from that unsettling moment to, a very few hours later, a beautifully composed, astonishingly intimate, deeply felt performance that stunned its small, fortunate, utterly captivated audience (myself included), is a blur in my recollection. But that journey captures so many things that I now know and cherish about Jo, and about her signature performance.

Constantly oscillating between fragility and robustness, there is a level of presence in Jo—a fierce vibration of energy and psychic sensitivity—that feels almost supernatural, but is also profoundly human. Not a transcendence, but a kind of transpondence: a remarkable alertness to the signals alive in the room, the traces, the ghost whispers, invisible but palpable as a prickling on the skin, a shimmering in the mind. This mode of presence is the very essence of theatre as a social and political and spiritual act: but I've seldom seen it enacted, embodied, with such absolute fidelity.

What I remember just as clearly, though, is Jo staying with us in the tiny flat that we'd rented down the road from the theatre; the conviviality of decent wine (she insisted on that!) and good companionship, generous laughter and unguarded conversation. And behind it all, the smell of fresh-baked bread, specially made for the evening show. I think perhaps only a female Jesus—a grandmotherly Jesus—would bake her own bread.

Jo is definitely in my all-time top two Jesuses.

Queen Jesus Goes to Brazil

The Gospel was first performed in Brazil in English at the FIT-BH international theatre festival in Belo Horizonte in May 2016. A month later, the Brazilian production O Evangelho Segundo Jesus, Raihna do Céu premiered in Londrina and would go on to be performed over 200 times in major festivals and venues across Brazil, selling out wherever it went. The play has faced huge opposition in Brazil, the country with the highest murder rate for queer and trans people in the world. Performances have been cancelled. The cast have received death threats. Simultaneously, the play has helped to change the landscape of theatre in Brazil, becoming a way to celebrate its rich, vibrant trans culture as well as a focus of discussion about censorship and the limits of art.

Diego Bagagal

Lisbon-based non-binary, interdisciplinary artist, and founder of Madame Teatro. Diego was part of the curatorship of the FIT-BH international festival in Belo Horizonte in 2016

It was in Edinburgh in 2015. I remember entering a small room, which was once used for veterinary anatomy classes. There was a place in the front row. I sat down. I did not know exactly what to expect. I had heard it was good.

Suddenly, Jo Clifford came in. A deep silence settled. There was a mountain in her. Before uttering any sound, she was already speaking, her deep voice projecting into the space like an enchantment. She hypnotised me.

This vocal power was the result of her encounter with the director Susan Worsfold. Susan created an atmosphere of real and artistic empowerment with and for Jo, who was fully present in her totality as a human being, merging the delicate lines between the human and the divine.

When Jo spoke her text, my masks start falling and I stopped pretending that I was a superhero. Jo was Jesus, and I was just a lion cub, who from an early age has never identified with any genre, and who was there in that veterinary room, on the other side of the Atlantic, alone. There was, in the air, an atmosphere that allowed Jo, from her reports of resilience and overcoming, to trigger within the audience a love so deep that it could kill her on the stage (which in fact almost happened in Belo Horizonte in 2016).

This performance opens you from the inside out, in a subtle and surgical act, without pain. The *Queen Jesus* team brought a new paradigm of Jesus, now without the cross. I remember that in the final scene of the mass I was holding hands with Jo, who by that time was already my Queen Jesus. I was looking up as if I were in front of my greatest idol, trying to contain my crying.

When I left, I cancelled the other pieces that I was going to see that day and returned to the hotel, and only then I cried. I cried with love. I understood, at that moment, that of all the performances I had seen, if I had to choose one, that would be it. I knew that this performance would reverberate very well in Belo Horizonte, which is very politically engaged with active and fruitful queer and feminists movements in the arts and politics.

Arriving at the festival, I suffered boycotts and prejudice in the final decision, but I fought, and in the end, I had to choose one... We, from Belo Horizonte, were ready to experience Love with Queen Jesus.

And so it was. Amen!

Juli Azevedo

Translator and field producer at the FIT-BH international festival in 2016. Juli looked after Jo, Susan, Annabel and Jak throughout their stay in Belo Horizonte. Her skills and caring nature were invaluable when Jo fell ill with a heart complaint was admitted to hospital. Juli has been a lifelong friend ever since

My first encounter with Queen Jesus was a gift from the universe. When I was assigned as the translator and field producer of Queen Jesus at 2016 FIT-BH, little did I know our relationship would evolve from professional to a strong bond of sisterhood.

The delicacy and beauty of *The Gospel According to Jesus, Queen of Heaven*, the odd rehearsal hours, the fear of an imminent uproar from religious fanatics, and, most of all, the collapse of Jo on the first five minutes of the last show brought us together forever.

After Jo fell ill, the seven-day stay at Vera Cruz Hospital in Belo Horizonte was a hard and worrying time but it was definitely one of the most touching human experiences I have had. The bond formed at that time became even stronger when, in the same year, I spent a couple of months in Edinburgh as a guest of Queen Jesus. When I left pretty little Edinburgh, I knew that time and distance would not weaken what had been built and we would enjoy the same warmth and true friendship even if it took us years to meet again. And I knew it because true sisters' love can endure anything. Thank you all my beautiful and dearest *Queen Jesus* sisters.

Liliane Rebelo

Cultural manager in Scotland and Brazil. Lili was instrumental in helping Queen Jesus travel to and make connections with Brazil, championing the work as part of her roles in cultural organisations in Brazil and Scotland such as the British Council and Festivals Edinburgh

I encountered Queen Jesus at a table at the Traverse bar in the winter of 2013. I met Jo in a work trip—I was being introduced to Scottish playwrights for a project I managed. Her internal tone of voice was of fear and shyness, but I remember the feeling I had about her writing being powerful and liberating. Something I can't describe in words connected me to her and the work called *The Gospel According to Jesus, Queen of Heaven.*

I only saw Jo performing the play a year and a half later, but it was during that period I became closer to her and to the *Queen Jesus* team, as a friend and someone impacted by the work. I loved Jo and her text. I also started to deepen my understanding of transphobia in society—particularly in my home country of Brazil—and how dangerous it is for trans people. It is a deep sense of human value and love that the play brings to the surface, challenging perceptions and stigmas.

I felt I wanted to share that learning and love with others, and by introducing her work to friends I would support the movement. And so, I did. I asked a friend—Natalia Mallo, who would go on to translate and direct the play in Brazil—to go and see that play and meet Jo. Natalia was equally touched by it and started her own journey of experience with it, which was extraordinary and reverberating on so many levels. *Queen Jesus* was visibly a family at that moment.

The play has the power to affect people in so many ways, on different levels and depths. Every performance brings changes to the audience members and society, but above all, it shares messages of love and empathy. Over ten years, the work has transformed many people's lives (and certainly mine), but mostly it has reinvigorated the idea that theatre crates a space for dialogue and can make change happen.

Natalia Mallo

Translator and director of O Evangelho Segundo Jesus, Raihna do Céu. Natalia is a multi-artist and cultural entrepreneur born in Argentina and based in São Paulo, Brazil. She has twenty years of professional experience developing projects in the fields of music, performing arts and interdisciplinary practice. Her testimony was translated by Jo Clifford

It is still hard to measure the impact made by Jo Clifford's play *Queen Jesus* in Brazil. But many researchers and academics are already describing it as a work which has changed the history of Brazilian theatre.

It is a work that calls into question issues that until now have hardly been discussed. Issues such as trans representation in the arts; the importance of the quality of the representation of dissident identities and modes of existence in the theatre; the power art has to provoke reflection as it throws light on sensitive social issues and makes its aesthetic and political impacts on the world. The play points to a cultural change that urgently needs to happen in Brazil: a change in the social perception of bodies that are stigmatised, excluded from citizenship, and deprived of human rights. This is the situation of trans bodies.

Ever since it opened in English in Glasgow in 2009, and especially since the Portuguese version opened in the Festival of Londrina in 2016, this work has been provoking discussions that range from questions of representation to public policy, from the system of privilege affecting the cultural sector to the dissemination of new understandings of sexual and of gender diversity. The play is now the subject of analysis in academic work in different areas, it is debated among activists, it is discussed in town halls and in the National Congress in the context of public policy for the LGBT community, as well as in drama schools and in debates about the state control of artistic expression.

Jo Clifford's writing places the trans/travesti body and existence in the context of, and in dialogue with, Christian iconography; and in doing so, it creates an important conceptual dislocation. That body that society excludes, fetishises and attacks, that is absent from public discourse in the light of day, emerges as the protagonist and chronicler of their own story. It starts to occupy spaces that the public values, spaces like prestigious cultural institutions and international festivals. It appears in the media: in the country's main newspapers, on radio and on TV. It also becomes an important topic for debate on social networks. (After the first attempt at censorship, the play's Facebook page was accessed over a million times.)

The religious symbols the play employs in this conceptual dislocation became a profound challenge to established structures of power. The present complex and deeply polarised political situation in Brazil is seeing the rise of right-wing forces and fundamentalist discourses with hate-filled values. We have seen the appearance of a ferocious opposition to the play, often based on fake news and complete ignorance of the work, and attempts to suppress trans/travesti voices and remove their physical presence from the stage. This is fuelled by a movement which reflects and perpetuates historical and structural violence.

With their eyes on the past elections that placed an openly transphobic, fundamentalist and extreme-right wing individual, Jair Bolsonaro, in the presidency, extreme-right political groups, working in an alliance with neo-Pentecostal religious groups, politicians, members of the congress and of the government, conducted a crusade against the play. The methods they used and continue using include court orders, slanders, spreading fake news, threats of physical violence, and boycotting strategies (such as the mayor of Rio de Janeiro closing a cultural centre and cancelling an entire festival to disguise his censorship of the play).

These practices have the ultimate effect of threatening the autonomy of other arts practitioners and their capacity to take risks. They create self-censorship and revive old methods of censorship in institutions; they instil fear in curators, programmers and sources of funding when they are making judgements about other possibly controversial themes that need spaces and resources in order for the public to see them.

At the same time, and even before these massive controversies, the play has achieved great success with the public. It has been performed almost two hundred times in two years, and has attracted huge crowds in every venue. Up to now, tickets sell out wherever it goes. The piece has been performed in every single international festival in Brazil, besides reaching Northern Ireland, Cape Verde, Argentina, Uruguay and Germany. It has been performed in theatres, in cultural centres, and in museums, as well as in homeless shelters, prisons, refuges, churches and even on the streets.

To go and see the play has become a political act. It is both an act of resistance against censorship and a collective action of solidarity. It has created networks of mutual support and help, and inspired new models of distribution of artistic work. It has activated a collective movement of affirmation that counters contemporary dystopian narratives and creates new forms of resistance.

Every single banning order has been reversed, on the grounds that they are anti constitutional. Every time attempts have been made to censor it, the forces of censorship have come out of the process demoralised, defeated and denounced by important sectors of society, including lawyers, academics, theologians, members of the artistic community, and international cultural and human rights organisations.

In the middle of this confusing picture of violence and struggle, of setbacks and victories, it is possible now to see several crucial cultural changes. No-one now can talk about art in Brazil without also mentioning representation. No-one can talk about democracy and state of law unless art can be created in freedom, even if it causes dissension and controversy.

It has never been more evident that we need to create and strengthen spaces for healthy dialogue. Plays like this are the necessary means to alert the public, the government and other public institutions of the urgency of this need. The structural inequality within the social fabric is no longer sustainable, as this play's long journey demonstrates with utter clarity.

At the same time, its discourse is not based on discord or on a black and white value system of denunciation. On the contrary, through revealing in a body of flesh and blood the reality of oppression, it throws life into sharp relief and is an invitation to imagine a different world. A world of pardon and acceptance where many perspectives, identities, genders and sexualities can live together.

Gabi Gonçalves

Producer of Queen Jesus BR and director of Núcleo Corpor Rastreado

B.Q.J. A.Q.J.

Before Queen Jesus, After Queen Jesus.

It was summer of 2015 when Natalia Mallo came to me to tell me about this text.

We had already worked together—we were already partners—but on that particular day, I felt a strange force in the conversation. I was extremely impacted by what she told me about the text and how it touched her. When I read it, I promptly decided that we would produce it.

The text: *The Gospel According to Jesus, Queen of Heaven* by Jo Clifford.

Natalia, who translated, adapted and directed it, had already found the actress Renata Carvalho, who identifies as travesti. Renata has described this elsewhere: "Travesti is a Latin American identity, most commonly found in Brazil. It is usually linked to poverty. The travesti, the trans woman and the cisgendered woman all belong to the same gender—the feminine. We understand ourselves and we express ourselves through that phenotype, and that is how we wish to be treated.

"However, we are not women and we are certainly not men. We are travesti. And I say this because gendered language, for a travesti, is very important, and in my country we often suffer the discomfort and indignity of people insisting on referring to us in the masculine. We are 'she.'

"I am a travesti. And to be a travesti in Brazil is a political act."

When I met Jo, she too was presented to me as a dissident body, the body of a practicing Christian trans woman, who used the theatre and its inexhaustible source of affections to reconcile her identities.

And all this has its own value, its own weight, and I knew I could not take a step back!

I felt that it would not work to produce this play using the production strategy I was accustomed to. I knew that *Queen Jesus* had the potential to generate a movement, but within the cisgendered logics of producing, *Queen Jesus* simply wouldn't happen—I knew that people would say 'no' to it. I had to find ways of producing the text myself without external resources. I knew that only believing and believing *very* much in a work like this, in what exactly it means in terms of challenging the establishment, something would be possible. The way was to help put this text out there in the world and wait for the devolutive judgement and—why not?—the silencing, the censorship.

But for good or ill, I could not imagine what was to come.

For a year, we produced the piece calmly, which is a paradox when it comes to the reality of professional production: the pragmatism and liquidity of our relationships, deadlines, meetings, encounters, and all the details lost along the way. It was twelve months of testing and learning. The development period was dictated by the money available. After all, it was money that I did not have. I had to find the means to invest in this endeavour, saving money here and there, although we knew that *Queen Jesus* would debut anyway at the Londrina international festival.

The text and its production created a special moment between Natalia, Renata and me. We had time to produce, to rehearse and find the place of Jesus in our lives, and also in the text itself, allowing it to shift geographically to inhabit our lives in Brazil. Our partnership gradually established a milestone in my perception: before and after Queen Jesus. Before and after my meeting with them and with the text. *Queen Jesus* changed my way of looking at the world, of producing art, and understanding the political force of my work. Until then, I was still looking at my work as the result of intuition, but today I am sure that I'm a completely different cultural agent than I was four years ago.

Queen Jesus, incarnated by Renata Carvalho, is a person who teaches so much. I learned to perceive my place of privilege. I learned to look at all the structural issues into which, however much I struggle, I am inserted.

I learned that maybe the best way is not to fight, but to keep walking towards these places, real and imaginary, that portray and enhance those "speaking standpoints" which are usually invisible and silenced.

From the very first show, we went through a series of 'no's, censorship, lynchings. It had a unique impact in our lives. When I look at this work, the vastness and permanence of it, I see all that Renata has gone through and what she has found in reading, in studying, in books, in her re-existence. I call the attention of all who read this testimony to to the fact that Brazil is the country that kills the most LGBT people in the world.

To be part of making *The Gospel According to Jesus, Queen of Heaven* is to assume responsibility to alert and inform people that "gender theory is neither destructive nor indoctrinating: it simply seeks a form of political freedom"—in the words of Judith Butler.

Despite the pain and fear this production brought to us all, *Queen Jesus* also brought me the greatest greatness I could receive—which is the capacity to see the other's truth.

Listen.

Leave the front line.

Get out of the way. Give space for othered bodies to own their narrative, their protagonism.

I learned, I am learning and I will keep learning.

I feel honoured, glorified, chosen by this work and the innumerable lessons that came to me through this extremely human, transcendental experience.

It all starts here.

Natalia Mallo, Renata de Carvalho, Jo Clifford, Susan Worsfold, Annabel Cooper and Liliane Rebelo—thank you very much.

Renata Carvalho

Renata performs as Queen Jesus in O Evangelho Segundo Jesus, Rainha do Céu. Renata is an actress, director, playwright and transpologist (trans anthropologist) based in Sao Paulo. She is also founder of MONART (National Movement of Trans Artists), "Trans Representativity Manifesto" (which aims at trans artists playing trans characters) and COLLECTIVE T (the first art collective formed entirely by trans artists in Brazil). Her testimony was translated by Jo Clifford

"Transbiography," the post says, and they are looking for two trans actresses.

There is an email.

In reply, they ask for a video with a reading of a certain text. It is the beginning of the play, and also the beginning of my story with the play.

There isn't any more information about the name of the play, who wrote it, how many characters it has, or what it is about. On first reading, I notice something religious about it. When I read it again, that impression grew.

I learn the extract, put on a gold sequin dress I'd worn in a play once, and ask a friend, Zé Carlos, to film me on my mobile. And I send it off.

Even though the email asked for a neutral reading, I do it with a certain feeling. (It's an audition, after all.) And after a few days, I send another email offering to do another in case they don't like the one I've sent.

It's very rare that opportunities come up for trans actresses. In the very few auditions that there are for trans characters, we're always turned down with a variety of excuses. We end up with tiny roles, without proper stories. And it is always the cisgendered artists that are chosen for the trans roles.

Even after twenty years as a professional, I'm not getting work as an actress. At this time, I've been working as a hairdresser for seven years. That is the only way I can pay the bills and keep working in the theatre after three years working as a prostitute. In Brazil, 90% of travestis and trans women are forced to work as prostitutes.

A few days later, my friend Leo Nicoletti is at a play at the Edinburgh Festival Fringe and comes out feeling very moved. He talks to other people at the festival. One of them is Natalia Mallo, who says she is going to produce this same play in Brazil, and that she has already chosen the trans actress to play Jo's part.

He immediately says that he knows the ideal actress for the role.

Natalia says "Who?" and he says—"Renata Carvalho, an actress from Santos."

"It's her that we've chosen," Natalia replies.

Leo sends me a message: "You're the one who's been chosen."

Natalia sends me an email making an appointment. That week, she is going to be in Santos so we can meet each other.

I wear blow-dried blonde hair (carefully dyed), tinted eyebrows, painted nails, earrings, a long orange skirt, and a white tank top a bit low cut to show off my breasts.

We go to the Japanese restaurant next door to Natalia's hotel. We're opposite the beach, and it's there—in the middle of sushis, introductions, sashimis and a bit of talk about the thesis of the play—that Natalia puts a brown envelope on the table.

"This is the script of *The Gospel According to Jesus, Queen of Heaven* by Jo Clifford. You're my Jesus of Nazareth. It's a monologue. You OK with that?"

Another monologue? I thought. I already had a monologue I'd been performing for three years—*Inside Me Lives Another*. In it, I tell the story of my life and my trans identity.

And then I got a fright. Religion + Jesus + travesti? In Brazil?

I pick up the envelope. I put more soy sauce on my sushi, and I say bye bye to my blonde hair.

When I get home, I can't stop reading the script. Once, twice, three times... it moves me to the core of my being.

On the 7th of June, 2015, in the nineteenth LGBT Pride Parade in Sao Paulo, the biggest of its kind in the world, the trans woman Viviany Beleboni appears on one of the floats nailed to the cross, looking like an image of the crucified Christ, with a crown of thorns, body make-up representing the wounds, and above her head a placard reading "No more LGBT hatred." Viviany performs like this to draw attention to the constant murders, physical assaults and acts of violence suffered by Brazil's LGBTQI+ population.

But then she herself becomes the target of attacks on the Internet, death threats, threats of lynching and group assaults. Fundamentalist Christians and politicians demonstrate their loathing of that "perverse comparison." She is constantly attacked and her act, and the attacks on her, become world news.

They understand nothing.

Every 19 hours, Brazil kills an LGBTQI+ person.

Brazil is the country that kills the most travestis and transsexual people in the world.

Brazil is the country responsible for 40% of trans murders in the whole world.

The normal life expectancy in Brazil is 75. The average life expectancy of a travesti in Brazil is 35. We are not allowed to be middle aged, and we are not allowed to get old.

In one of the meetings we have in Santos, Natalia brings along Gabi Gonçalves. She comes to a rehearsal and decides to produce the show with her company Núcleo Corp Rastrado, and also act as assistant director.

That September, I stop being a hairdresser.

Natalia says I will have to dance in one scene. I say, "That'll be the last scene that's ready then." I don't have a body aware of being able to dance. I don't have an expressive body.

On the 8th of February, 2016, the samba school Estação Primeira de Mangueira begins to parade down the avenue, dancing a samba in honour of the singer Maria Bethânia. I'm a fan of hers and a fan of that samba school and it was my birthday, and I go to join the parade with the script in my hand.

While I am waiting for the dancers to reach the street, I study the script. And then all the while I'm dancing the samba, and singing the samba, and so moved by the samba, I'm looking at the script. And I'm remembering that I need to dance in a scene, and there I am dancing the samba, the text in my hand, looking at the scene with the dance in it.

"Don't mess with me because I am the daughter of Oyá..."

And so dancing to the drums of the Mangueira brings the play's first scene to life.

Is there any popular dance that could be more Brazilian?

Natalia says she sees a scene in which I change my costume. I'll have to be in panties on stage, and more than once I think: in every play, directors want to show my body. Preferably naked.

In one of the rehearsals, I ask her why this will be necessary. She says: "Because your body is political."

I never forget that. And now, as an actress, I need to find the reason for that change.

We do some open rehearsals for friends and acquaintances, and in these rehearsals I wear a long black dress that looks a bit faded. I have bare feet and carry a dark-blue Adidas bag. The original idea is for a sandy floor, and a Jesus who is quite detached from the feminine, conveying something close to gender neutrality.

For a rehearsal in Santos that takes place in a flat belonging to a friend of Natalia and Gabi, I ask two of my friends to come along, Junior and Kadu. It is then I notice I'm not happy performing dressed like that. I just don't see her that way. I want her to look more convincing and have everything that is needed for that to happen. The rehearsal is a failure.

In all the readings I do afterwards—the research on religion, Catholicism, the biographies of Jesus—the thing that concerns me more than anything is how to 'translate' this text for the reality of being travesti, and everything that goes with it. The physicality of being travesti. The essence of being travesti. And to find a way of making this a Brazilian story.

Each time we meet, and each time we rehearse, we work on the text, we discuss the text, scene by scene. But the Brazilian travesti are not in the image and not in the body of that Jesus: a simpler Jesus, a Jesus without makeup and in open-toed sandals. That Jesus is a white feminist cisgendered image in opposition to the cult of feminine stereotypes. And that's all valid, but contradicts what it means to be travesti. Feminine attributes were always within white feminists' reach. For us travestis, they were fiercely denied us:

Roses, lilacs, dolls, earrings, makeup, high heels, dresses, skirts, bras, panties, painted nails, plucked eyebrows, to have long hair, to cross one's legs…

As I go through the process of 'translating' this text and this story into a Brazilian reality, I keep asking: who would this Brazilian travesti Jesus be?

Jo Clifford, Susan Worsfold, and Annabel Cooper arrive in Brazil. The exchange between us three becomes fundamentally important. We travel together, and we do a rehearsal with them.

In conversation with Jo—in a mix of English, Portuguese and gestures—I explain my insecurities about portraying Jesus, and of my desire to put the travesti body in the story and reflect the reality of Brazilian life.

Jo patiently says to me: "You are Jesus, because you are the one portraying her. I do her my way because I am a different person. You must do her your way."

It feels like we have known each other for years.

I'd been researching the trans body since 2007, when I became a voluntary preventative health worker for the health department of my native city, Santos, on the coast of São Paulo. I was working in the field of HIV/AIDS, hepatitis and tuberculosis, and working specifically with travestis and trans women working as prostitutes. My travesti perception began in that year. I call this study 'transpology,' which is to say trans anthropology. And I discovered myself to be a 'transpologist,' a trans anthropologist, focusing on the arts.

I go back to Natalia and Gabi with photos and newspaper articles to introduce them to Indianare Alves Siqueira and Luana Muniz, two travestis who live in Rio. Their photos show two blonde travestis in full makeup, each one with the characteristics said to be feminine in their clothes, in their accessories, mannerisms, in their physicality and their way of speaking.

Luana Muniz was an LGBTQIA+ activist, prostitute, and someone who took part in a project that prepared travestis and transsexuals for the conventional job market. She welcomed travestis and transexuals, prostitutes and HIV positive people to her mansion in Lapa. She was the 'Queen of Lapa' who handed out clothing and food to people living on the streets, and who came to be known nationally by the slogan "A travesti is not a disaster zone," and who died at the age of 56 from a heart attack.

Indianare Siqueira is a whore, a vegan, and a militant for human rights and the rights of LGBTQIA+ people, prostitutes, and HIV positive people, of the homeless, people living on the street, but mostly of the rights of 'transvestigendered' people—a word she invented to include travestis, trans women and trans men. She set up the PreparaNem programme to prepare people for higher-education entrance exams. She squatted in empty buildings in Rio de Janeiro, and she created the Casa Neo for trans people thrown out of the family home. Indianare also spent time in Santos, my city, where she slept on the street, worked as a prostitute, and founded the Philadelphia NGO group to combat HIV/AIDS. At the that time, Santos was considered a global capital of the disease.

When I knew them, both were women over forty years old.

I want to show Natalia and Gabi that it isn't just a question of looking pretty on stage, but of living through the process of constructing the travesti identity.

"They are my Brazilian Jesus," I tell them.

From that meeting on, a new show begins to develop.

The travesti language—the pajubá—travesti mannerisms, high heels, earrings, heavy makeup and false eyelashes begin to give shape to this new Brazilian travesti Jesus.

My gold sequin dress finds its way back into rehearsals.

The first thing I needed to do in the process of constructing this travesti physicality was to get to know my own body. However much the big majority of trans people are obsessed with changing our bodies, we don't usually truly look at them. We don't get on well with mirrors. Who can look after this body which is always rejected? Which is laughable? Hateful? A constant target?

Gisele Calazans and Fabricio Licursi teach me how to stretch and extend my body. We need to know how much space we take up in the world. They put me in contact with my gesture, my movement, my muscles, and my bones.

Another huge question for trans people and for me is the voice. The voice of the travesti is so often the butt of derisive laughter. Patricia Anoniazi, a vocal coach, teaches me to breathe on stage, to control my breath, to make my voice sound better to the audience, and above all allows me to discover how to be calm on stage. How to warm up so I can walk on stage without trembling. How to learn to like my voice for being unique and for being mine.

Being with these women is transformative.

Natalia and Gabi give me all the technical support I need to perfect my voice and my interpretation, my moves and my gestures.

Natalia wants a song in the performance, and I introduce her to 'Um beijo pras travestis' ('Give the travestis a kiss') by the travesti singer MC Xuxu.

For the scene with the costume change, one day when I was looking up trans musicians I come across the song 'A pele mars find' ('The thinnest skin') by Salada das Frutas, with the trans vocalists Liniker, Raquel Virginia, and Assucena Assucena. The scene would begin after the line "And we blunder about..."

The "blunder" of travestis is what happens to us: when 90% of us are thrown out of our homes when we are between 12 and 14 years old, when it's only the street corners that welcome us with open arms. In my case, this was the journey towards prostitution. At that moment in the play, Jesus shows her travesti physicality through the industrial silicone in her breast implants and in her bottom.

Just as we all know the end of this story, I think that Jesus knew what was going to happen to him, and she knows too. So what does she do? She walks towards the cross, looking fabulous in her high heels, touching up her lipstick and mascara, in her painted nails and her gorgeous sequin dress... Openly and courageously is how she goes.

To protect my safety, the poster and publicity photos do not show my face. One phrase sums up the play and almost becomes a slogan: "What if Jesus came to us now as a travesti?"

That is the provocation that politicians and religious people need; and it also wins us likes, following, and supporters.

Gabi had managed to get the show programmed for the International Londrina Festival (or FILO) and we arrived there on the 26th of August, 2016. We were due to perform on August 27, 28 and 29th, in the old chapel of the UEL (Londrina State University) and all the shows were sold out.

The festival told us that they were under great pressure to cancel the performances. Politicians, religious organisations, religious institutions and traditional churchgoers were all petitioning the university principal. We knew that attacks on the play had already begun on social media, condemning the piece without having seen it or read it. But we knew that the Internet belongs to everyone and no-one.

A candidate for the city council, one Felipe Barrios (who was elected and who is now a federal deputy) made a video attacking the play and asking for the authorities to ban it. What's more, he comes to the venue as it was being set up and films himself asking: "Can Jesus be a homosexual?" Viviana Gelpi, the stage manager, and Juliana Augusta, the lighting designer, began to remonstrate. He keeps filming them and they begin a discussion. He posts it on the Internet calling them "hysterical feminazis".

The debate heats up. The pressure on the university increases. My social media begins to receive hate mail, threats of beating, of stoning, of being shot on stage or when I set foot in the city. I find out that one of the men most attacking me online is a well-known weapons collector.

I call a travesti friend of mine, the actress and activist Mel Campus, asking for reinforcements. Mel calls out the whole LGBTQIA+ movement of Londrina and the surrounding area.

On the 27th, the day of the opening, we are denied access to the chapel for "reasons of security," according to the university. Our performance is instead transferred to one of the campus lecture halls, almost tripling the seating capacity.

We hire bodyguards.

I am staying in a house which gives me a view of the chapel and of the new venue. Looking out the window, we see a man hidden behind a tree watching the entrance to the chapel. It is the weapons collector. The police remove him from the campus.

The public is waiting outside the chapel. Beside them is a small group of eight to twelve frightened looking people who have come to protest. To protest against what?

As night falls on the campus, about three hundred people process silently, holding candles, to the new venue.

Women stand at the auditorium entrance: activists, some pregnant, some with young children, who had come to affix placards to the entrance against transphobia and in support of freedom of expression, and to make a human shield around the entrance to prevent anyone attacking me.

In my black dress, with my makeup, my painted nails, a trench coat and a handbag and drinking a fizzy drink through a straw: that's how Jesus reached the entrance of the theatre.

There's security guards in the packed auditorium and, as I make my entrance, I feel this overwhelming need to vomit. A man in a white t-shirt sits on the front row and I can see myself being sick all over him. I think: I didn't come here to be ill and not perform the play after all that's happened. I breathe, I breathe, I tell myself I just want to burp and I get to the end. Then I run out into the garden at the back and vomit as I've never vomited before.

And that's how we open: with massive press coverage, my social networks swarming with attacks, and a run of full houses.

In the dressing room, I turn to everyone and say: "Welcome to transphobia."

Little did we know that this programme of welcome would be repeated over and over again, and with the same ingredients.

On the 27th of June, 2018, the programme for the Garanhuns Winter Festival is announced. On the 30th, we are withdrawn from the programme.

Artists' groups and LGBTQIA+ groups in the city get themselves organised to raise the funds to pay for us to perform independently. The goal is to raise six thousand reales. We raise twelve thousand.

On July 22nd, performing in the festival, the singer Daniele Mercury makes a public statement in our defence. She is attacked on social media.

On July 27th, our flight lands in Maceio—for security reasons, we've decided to land in another province. As soon as we land, we're told that a senior judge in the justice department of Pernambuco, Silvio Neves Baptista Filho, has ordered that the directors of the festival put the play back in their programme or face a fine of fifty thousand reales.

The festival no longer had a space for us to perform in, so they were asking if we could put on an extra performance in our own space. In return, they'd pay for the equipment and for more security guards.

At ten o'clock we hit the road. It takes three and a half hours to get to Garanhuns. It's very cold. We reach the hotel at two o'clock, when there was a meeting scheduled between us, the festival organisers and the state government. The festival organisers, FUNDARPE, had appealed the judicial decision that they re-programme our performance. Cowards. One of the FUNDARPE officials begins the meeting by saying he doesn't understand why they are being called "censors," and that's why they are appealing to the judges.

What a shitface, I think, and he's going on and on... I stop him.

"I don't care what you think," I say, "and I don't care what FUNDARPE thinks, or the mayor's office, or the ministry of culture, or the secretariat. It doesn't interest me. If you were called 'censors,' its because you are censors. And I advise you not to come to any of the performances because you won't be welcome. What concerns me is my safety and the safety of the audience, and I want to know how the people who want to see the show are going to be informed. That's what matters, not what you think."

I'm not allowed to walk on the streets. We're taken to the venue that's been hired. I'm given a bullet proof vest. I discard it.

At twenty past five, the first performance begins. A full house. The performance lasts just over an hour and there are no problems. People are already queueing outside for the next show, which is scheduled for nine o'clock.

While I'm talking to some journalists, there's a loud noise.

I turn round. The space is full of smoke. People are rushing about. It's a bomb.

I'm surrounded by security guards and taken inside.

Nothing is found inside. They search the surrounding area. It gets colder. It starts to rain.

Officials from the Justice Ministry appear to forbid the performance. This is an order from the judge Roberto Silva Maia, responding to a petition from the Organisation of Evangelical Pastors of Garanhuns and District.

We decide to go ahead anyway, as an independent company.

In my dressing room, I am told they are taking down the lights and the sound.

When I get to the auditorium, the chairs have already been stacked up, the lights and sound disconnected, and I hear the three employees who are doing this (and I name them: Marcus, Nena and Diego) insulting our show and everyone involved in it. An important detail: inside a space that *we* have rented.

I go up to the three of them and shout in their faces: "Fascists, sell-outs, censors!"

One by one, I begin to knock down the heaps of piled up chairs.

I hear someone say: "Hold her down!"

I say, still knocking the chairs over: "Why? Is there a law that gives you the right to arrest a travesti for knocking chairs over?"

I stand on the white chairs and shout: "These are clouds! I am Jesus! I am in Heaven!"

When our stage manager Jimmy Wong takes me by the arm and says "Quick, Renata, everyone's leaving," I think: "I need our audience."

I run to the main door. They try to stop me leaving—I take no notice, I run out the door, I shout to the queue (by this stage about three or four hundred strong): "They want to censor us again. I need you to enter the space as fast as you can."

I get back inside and I ask the eight security guards we have hired to let the audience enter. For security reasons, it is necessary for them to be searched. I ask them to start the process.

I run to the highest part of the space and I shout: "This is the travesti play, fuck it. They think travesti is the same as shit. If they want a show they'll get a travesti show, here's a travesti!"

I was yelling at the top of my voice. I was beside myself.

Then I see they're still trying to stop the audience coming in. There's a wall being formed by security guards, headed up by Nena, on the telephone.

I ask: "Who's stopping people coming in?"

She says: "The military police."

I reply: "Where is the injunction?"

I try to open the entrance door. They stop me. I push the security guards aside and I push the door wide open, shouting at the audience to occupy the space.

The security guards try to forcibly pull me from the entrance. One of them throws a punch.

Chico Ludermir, a local activist, says! "Don't do that. She's the actress in the play."

The public all start shouting together: "Down with censorship! Fascists!"

All is tumult and confusion: but the public are occupying the space.

I discuss with Jimmy about where to place the security guards, scattered among the audience, but in the end we just leave the audience without being searched, in the hope that the audience around me will protect me.

Now the officials demand documentation that we have hired the space, the lighting and sound equipment.

A lawyer appears from out of the audience and provides a moment of distraction.

We take advantage of this and start the performance without lights or sound. The audience greet me with loud applause. I am lit by cell phones. Before I start the play, I throw Marcus and Diego out the space.

Just after we've begun, the woman who owns the venue interrupts by saying that we need to come out from under the shelter the FUNDARPE paid for and stop sitting on their chairs.

The audience all move out into the cold and the rain. They help me move the portable altar. In spite of the cold and the pouring rain, everyone stays. The performance restarts.

The FUNDARPE employees start to take out the rest of the space in the noisiest way they can. The audience reacts, but they don't stop. I stop the performance and walk up to them. I ask them to stop work and wait till the end of the show. They ignore me.

I ask them: "Have you no respect? Do you want me to start knocking over the chairs again?"

They don't stop.

I shout "That's enough!" and start knocking over chairs.

The audience comes up to them. Confusion. Someone tells them to stop. The audience come up to the employees and escort them to the door. They are thrown out of the space.

The second performance continues, and the audience sing the songs for us a cappella.

Later, another judicial order obliges us to be put back into the festival programme.

We are still receiving invitations to perform. Wherever the show goes, it is a success both with the critics and with the public. Looking back over everything that's happened, we now know that the censorship the show suffered did it a lot of good, and was good for my career, too; and that because of it, news of the production spread abroad and has taken us to places we never imagined ourselves going.

But to go through this, to be constantly attacked, to maintain physical and mental health through it all, and to resist physical illness is not an easy task. To be censored, to be not allowed to perform, means to be without work.

The play has raised questions that have never been discussed before. It has challenged the institutional structures of religious, political, and judicial institutions. It has stripped away transphobic masks. It has suffered threats, censorship, and violations of a frequency and savagery that have never before occurred, even during the dictatorship.

Why so much fear of a play?

All that hatred, all that rage, all those attacks, are directed against the word 'travesti' and everything it represents.

Jesus is the image and representation of all humanity, except us trans people. We have an inappropriate body, a sexualised body, a fetishised body, a body possessed by demons and so, apparently, we cannot represent someone as pure as Jesus. The problem arises from the image, and the imagery created in the collective imagination about the travesti. Created by the social construction of what it means to be a travesti, the carnivalised media construction of what it means to be travesti, a pathological construction, the product of transphobic mockery and transphobic narratives constructed by art, medicine, religion, the judiciary and the media.

We need to change this imagery and transform this social construction. We need to humanise, calm and make natural the way cisgendered people see us and perceive us and respond to our presence.

This can only be done through trans representation, with our bodies being present in theatre spaces, and public spaces in general, so that cis people can learn to live with trans bodies. Because through living and being together that we can demystify all these fantasies attached to our bodies, our identities and our lives.

And now we know the transformative power of theatre and the power of art. We know how it can open minds and hearts and throw light on the questions that matter.

As my fellow native of Santos, the playwright Plinio Marcos says: "The artist is the reporter in a dark time."

In this play, I found my calling as an artist, and it has given me the foundation and the strength to never leave this vocation. I never knew or even imagined that in 2009 this play was being written for me.

Thank you Jo Clifford.

Thank you Natalia Mallo.

Thank you Gabi Gonçalves.

Thank you Núcleo Corpo Rastreado.

Thank you everyone who came to the performances.

Thank you everyone who struggled to prevent the play being censored.

Thank you Salvador, Rio de Janeiro, Garanhuns, Recife and Pernambuco for all your acts of resistance.

Thank you to all the festivals and SESC arts centres who welcomed us and refused to give way to pressure.

Thank you for all the audiences who were there and resisted for more than two hundred performances, and for every audience member who will still come.

Because the struggle continues.

Welcome to the traviarcado, where every body is natural.

Blessings. Farewell...

Nik Williams

Project manager at Scottish PEN, an organisation that defends the freedom of writers and readers

What do we hold as sacred? In many ways, this question frames everything we do—what we hold dear, what we protect, who we amplify, and inversely who we attempt to ignore or silence. This is also the question that Jo Clifford positions at the heart of her pioneering performance, *The Gospel According to Jesus, Queen of Heaven*. The question also comes with an implicit challenge—how do we bring more people with us when we define what is sacred? How can we champion the ignored, silenced and marginalised and ultimately renew our concept of humanity as something that celebrates our shared, varied and noisy world as opposed to limiting it?

Scottish PEN exists as part of a global community of writers who fight to protect free expression to ensure everyone can speak out and speak up. I first encountered Jo Clifford's work when I was in Lviv for the 2017 PEN International Congress, where PEN centres from around the globe came together to share ideas for protecting at-risk writers, discuss key challenges and renew our commitment to free expression. I was sitting on my hotel room bed about to head to the main congress hearing, when I received an email from a Scottish PEN trustee who informed me that a performance of *Queen Jesus* was banned at SESC Jundiai in Sao Paulo in Brazil, and that the ban was supported by representatives from the Catholic and Evangelical churches. I wished I could be surprised by the reaction towards the play, but I knew anything that engages with trans rights or represents trans people has faced immediate condemnation, abuse, opposition and at times violence, especially in Brazil. According to the Trans Murder Monitoring project, just under 3000 trans people were murdered in the decade ending 2018; Brazil is the most dangerous place for trans people, with the highest trans murder rate in the world. And

Jo was doing more than telling the story of a trans person: she was reimagining Jesus as a trans person, expanding the ideal of the sacred.

Working with Jo and PEN International gave us a shocking insight into the threats facing both the play and everyone involved in the production. Venues were being boycotted and performances cancelled, radio interviews with prominent clergymen condemned the morals behind the play with no one from the play able to respond, injunctions were shared, car tires were slashed, YouTube films with death threats were produced, bomb threats were called into participating venues, causing armed-police raids just before curtain up. In the face of these threats, it was hard not to see silence as something safer, something easier. But then, of course, what is left unsaid? Whose voice, identity and history is ignored? *The Gospel According to Jesus, Queen of Heaven* epitomises the power of art, why it is a threat to the status quo and those unprepared to defend their opinions, and why it is important for us to stand against threats of censorship or violence.

As a result of our work and the threats facing the play, Jo Clifford and the play's director and translator, Natalia Mallo, were included in the PEN International 2017 case list—Jo is, in fact, the sole Scot and one of only two British nationals on the list. Last year, alongside English PEN, PEN International, Wales PEN Cymru and the global secretariats of the Writers in Prison Committee and the Women Writers Committee, Scottish PEN authored a letter to the then-UK foreign secretary, Jeremy Hunt, demanding that he engages with the Brazilian authorities to ensure the play could be performed unhindered. As Jair Bolsonaro, the new Brazilian president, has outlined a hard-line opposition to the LGBTQI community (once declaring he would prefer his son to be killed in a road accident than be gay), Jo's play is more important than ever, but also more threatened than ever before. I am writing this seven months after sending the letter to Jeremy Hunt about the threats to Jo Clifford, and we are yet to receive a response or acknowledgement. In 2019, Jeremy Hunt resigned.

In December 2018, I attended *The Gospel According to Jesus, Queen of Heaven* at the Traverse Theatre in Edinburgh. After our campaigning, I was delighted to finally see the play, but having been so focused on the forces that have attempted to silence it, I didn't know what to expect. The threats of violence and censorship and the inaction of the UK Government remained at the forefront of my mind as I took my seat around a long, white dining table adorned with candles, lengths of greenery, a white table cloth and a solitary loaf of bread in the centre. But as I watched it, I realised why churches and politicians had been afraid of the play—it was warm, funny but above all humane, seeing in biblical stories a chance to celebrate what unites us as opposed to what divides us. Beyond that, the play undermined the dehumanised discourse framing trans rights and did it with a smile, a slight laugh and a warm embrace. As I headed back for the train to Glasgow, part of me remained under the spell of the play, but I couldn't shake the knowledge that there are still forces fighting to ensure the play is never performed.

Scottish PEN will continue to support and defend Jo Clifford, Natalia Mallo and anyone involved in this important piece of art. When censorship succeeds, silence prevails, leaving democracy and the world around us a much more fragile and less welcoming place.

Spiritual Perspectives

Fiona Bennett

Minister of Augustine United Church, Edinburgh

The first time I encountered *Queen Jesus* was through reading the script. Our church (Augustine United Church in Edinburgh, where Jo is a member) planned to put on a performance of *Queen Jesus* as part of Pride. Given the horrific hatred *Queen Jesus* has received in Glasgow, Jo wanted me, as the minister, to read the script before we put it on. Reading the script, as someone who wrestles with and interprets scripture all the time, was delightful. Jo's sense of the nuance, honour and tension in the Biblical stories is very good, but reading the script is only a shadow of encountering it in performance.

For the Pride performance, we sat in a huge circle and Jo enabled us to meet Jesus in a new yet very familiar way. I have seen *Queen Jesus* performed five or six times now and each time is for me a fresh encounter with the living God.

What is amusing about *Queen* Jesus is how conventional it is! *Queen Jesus* offers us teaching and stories very much along the lines brother Jesus did. But her identity as a transwomen (and the glorious craft in the words and performance) make the story intimate, relevant and alive. After the first time I saw *Queen Jesus* performed I described it as a "devotional" piece, which in my mind is just exactly what it is. It is an expression of Jo's heartfelt spirituality and sits on the cusp of theatre as liturgy, inviting the audience to taste God's love and hope as Jesus revealed.

It fills me with deep joy to know that *Queen Jesus* has brought courage and acceptance to so many people in Scotland and across the globe. I am truly inspired by Jo's craft, tenacious vision, courage and boundless grace, which the Divine Spirit has woven into a tapestry for transformation through the devotional piece which is *The Gospel According to Jesus, Queen of Heaven.*

Zanne Domoney-Lyttle & Sarah Nicholson

Biblical Studies scholars at the University of Glasgow

We first properly encountered *Queen Jesus* when we invited Jo to perform her play at the University of Glasgow's memorial chapel in January 2019. We had read the script before, and we were excited to include the performance and a discussion with Jo as part of our honours class taught in Theology & Religious Studies at Glasgow, which focussed on themes of women, gender and sexuality in the Bible.

Jo's performance and class discussion was a powerful reminder to our students that there is no single way to read or interpret the Bible. Using her performance as a pedagogical approach also allowed our students to see how biblical texts can be opened up and re-framed outside of a heteronormative, patriarchal approach, which is something we often talk about but lack concrete examples of in class.

After the performance and Jo's class discussion, our students expressed considerable praise for the play and discussed how their understanding of the intersections between theology and gender had been both deepened and challenged by the performance. Aside from aiding our students in an academic capacity, it is also highly important to note that students valued the emotional aspect of *Queen Jesus*. For many, they noted that presenting a 'human' Jesus (as opposed to a spiritual or theological version of Jesus) helped to illuminate real-world issues of marginalisation and discrimination that trans communities face on a global level.

The work that Jo and her wonderful team continue to carry out is both vital and necessary to further highlight and examine the intersections of religion, gender binaries and spirituality which dominate so many lives. We are expressly grateful for her courage and willing to speak out on such issues and to demonstrate how we should all act as humans, regardless of gender, race, age, ethnicity or any other divisive rhetoric.

Maxwell Reay

Chaplain of the Department of Spiritual Care at the Royal Edinburgh Hospital.

I am a minister with Metropolitan Community Church and work for the NHS as a mental-health chaplain. In my work, I regularly work with folks from the LGBT community in hospital and community settings.

My role in the NHS is to support the spiritual care of people of any faith or no faith. This helps folks deal with issues of identity, meaning and purpose, connections to others, a sense of something greater outside themselves.

I spend a significant amount of time supporting those who have been damaged and hurt by homophobic and transphobic attitudes and behaviours. The mental health of LGBT folks is impacted negatively in a much greater way than the general population due to stigma, prejudice and violence.

Often this type of damage comes directly from churches and faith communities. In the Christian tradition, misinterpretations and theologically wrong interpretations of the Bible are often used as a weapon against trans folk. This is wrong and breaks my heart. It is so damaging to the core of who a person is and how they identify in the world. At worst, folks take their own lives. At best, folks find a way to cope.

Many people find healing and health through the arts. Art can be a wonderful coping mechanism. This means we need artists to take risks and share life experiences that are relevant and meaningful to those LGBT audiences.

Jo Clifford's play *Queen Jesus* has, over the last ten years, brought healing and health to many individuals and groups. I have witnessed this for myself with those I have worked alongside.

Jo is a role model for many trans and non binary folks and the honesty in her work has been so refreshing in a world that wants to silence the oppressed.

The tem-year anniversary performances will link the

communities of trans folks from the UK and Brazil. Being connected to our trans siblings in other countries is important. Sharing journeys across continents is also a powerful and positive way of telling the wider world that difference should be celebrated and not hidden.

Queer Perspectives

Jak Soroka

Associate artist for Queen Jesus Productions. Jak worked as a stage manager across productions in Brazil and the UK.

My first encounter with *Queen Jesus* was watching the film version of the show. I had just been invited to work on the performances in Brazil as stage manager and associate artist. When I think back, I really knew very little about it. I certainly had no idea how much a part of the team I would become, and how much the piece would become part of me. I just had a good gut feeling that it was something I wanted to be part of.

I remember Jo's voice, soothing, rich, and calm. Her face kind, eyes soft. The whole text rolled over me. Later that week, I would read the play and weep. I'm not of Christian faith, but to see our people written in to such iconic and sacred stories—places we have historically been banished from—felt momentous. Felt... weird. Do we belong here? Are we welcome? Why would we want to be, after centuries of exclusion, persecution and shaming? This is what floated in my head. In my body, I felt warm. I felt hopeful. And, despite only having met Jo a handful of times, I felt totally sure of going with *Queen Jesus* to the other side of the world.

Since that first encounter, I have seen Queen Jesus herself in person many times. I have laid tables for her in Elephant and Castle, moved chairs in a church in Hull, lit candles in a Brazilian museum... It's given me dear friends, and a team that feels like family. It's contributed to shaking up my beliefs on being religious and LGBTQ+ (spoiler: you can be both!) It's taught me that being gentle and welcoming can be just as radical as being loud and shocking.

The show touches me in a unique way when it's a majority queer and trans audience watching. I've seen how it burrows deep into a shared moment to plant a message—one that we always long to hear as folx marginalised because of who we are. That is: you are loved. You are accepted. All that you are is beautiful.

The stories of celebration, wisdom and care weave around a room and lift it, fill it with light. This has given me a most wonderful gift, every time: a place to belong.

James Morton

Campaigner, activist and Scottish Trans Alliance manager. STA works to improve gender identity and gender reassignment equality, rights and inclusion in Scotland.

I remember vividly the premiere of *Queen Jesus* in 2009 and how shaken and confused Jo seemed when she first relayed to me the denunciations and intense hostility being unexpectedly directed at her by protestors who had not even seen the play.

It can be so difficult to maintain resilience and self-confidence in the face of hatred, but Jo has been exemplary in responding with dignity, determination and compassion.

Every time the play is performed in the UK, trans people share with me the positive strength they and their loved ones draw from seeing it.

Following the news of the play's international performances has provided trans people in Scotland with a wider perspective and appreciation of trans activism in other cultures.

The play is not merely a moment of cultural significance, it is an ongoing source of sustenance and empowerment for diverse trans equality activism. Thank you Jo for sharing your energy and love with us.

James T. Harding

Publisher, editor and designer for Stewed Rhubarb

I was raised by a recovering Catholic who sent me to Protestant Sunday schools and told me it was all nonsense each week when I returned home. The results of this were an aesthetic appreciation for ceremony, a tendency to question authority, and a snooty distain for the type of evangelism that waves a tambourine. In other words, little more than spiritual trappings.

I have been blessed to see *Queen Jesus* in several of its different incarnations. It has changed much over the time I have been a part of its congregation, both in text and in presentation, but one thing has remained constant: the queer people in the audience. Sometimes it's literally the same people, who I recognise in the crowds at the book launch, the church, the festival, the theatre. Always, however, there is a glint of solidarity in people's eyes, a glimpse of a spiritual queer communion which is quite different from the community feeling of a pride event or the party atmosphere of a club.

This, for me, is the power of *Queen Jesus* incarnate: a spirituality which does better than merely tolerate queer people, it makes the queer part of us a source of spirituality and wisdom.

When I met Jo Clifford and saw her *Queen Jesus*, I experienced what it could mean, as a queer person, to lead a spiritual life. The Anglican Christianity I had been brought up with looked like a hollow shell in comparison.

I published a pamphlet of the play in July 2014, to coincide with the Fringe performance at the Just Festival. At the time, I was a semi-lapsed member of St John's the Evangelist, the host church of the Just Festival, and I felt deeply betrayed by their decision to cancel the play at short notice, and correspondingly grateful to St Mark's Unitarian Church for taking it on. It is not entirely fair of me, perhaps, but I have never attended a service at St John's since.

In April 2016, I published Natalia Mallo's translation of the play into Portuguese. It was an immense privilege to see Natalia's version in parallel with the English, and to learn from her about some of the cultural differences which led her to adjust parts of the text. She showed me how queerness can connect us across cultural boundaries in a way which respects the ways we are different, which doesn't find it necessary to homogenise what it means to be queer.

And then the reception of the play in Brazil reminded me, yet again, how much work there is to be done.

When Jo first started working with Stewed Rhubarb, we were a tiny outfit with no sales network to speak of and only nine publications to our name. Jo and the *Queen Jesus* team's ongoing faith in us has helped Stewed Rhubarb to grow—and given me a reason to grow it. As well as entrusting *Queen Jesus* to Stewed Rhubarb, Jo has contributed time and writing to anthologies I worked on in collaboration with LGBT Health and Wellbeing, *Naked Among Thistles* (2014, ed. Katherine McMahon & Alison Wren), and *The Gender Garden* (2016, ed. Katherine McMahon).

Stewed Rhubarb is still a tiny outfit as publishers go, but we are now bigger, stronger, and more connected. Crucially, I will now be able to make this book available almost worldwide, including in Brazil. It brings me great joy to know that this life-changing play will reach more English-speaking trans and queer people than ever before.

I say to them: Hello and welcome. And I hope you find what you seek here.

Ardel Haefele-Thomas

Chair of Lesbian, Gay, Bisexual, Transgender and Queer Studies at City College, San Francisco

I first encountered Jo Clifford and *The Gospel According to Jesus, Queen of Heaven* from one of my students in a global LGBTQ+ art and culture class. Charlie loves the theatre and for his presentation on an artist, he showed various clips of Jo Clifford. I could see right away what their immediate love was for this amazing playwright. As I listened to clips of *Queen Jesus*, I could not help being transported into my own past—as a young queer and trans person raised in the Bible Belt in Oklahoma in the US, I dreaded going to church, whether with my grandparents or my aunts and uncles. I dreaded it because hate was preached from the pulpit every week. I would sit there, crammed into my dress that was itchy, and wish I were back home in my shorts and t-shirt, and just suffer through some white male preacher going on and on about how someone like me was going to go to hell. Year after year, I had to sit in various churches and hear this. To the point that I walked away from Christianity entirely.

But I did not walk away from Jesus the prophet, nor did I walk away from messages of love coming from Jesus. I mean, there is something to be said for the fact that the first person Jesus appeared to after rising is a sex worker!

I sat in an inner urban clinic in San Francisco a few years ago, waiting for an HIV test. I was in the waiting room with several trans women—many of whom were homeless and many of whom did sex work. And all I could think about was that this waiting room is where I would find Jesus—not in the churches, preaching hate.

So, to sit in my class and watch the beautiful Jo Clifford present Jesus as a trans woman? Well, all I could think about was that the prophet would be proud—because Jesus is all of us. Jesus is a trans woman.

Thank you, Jo Clifford! Had I had your Jesus growing up, who knows—I might have become a preacher instead of a teacher...

Extracts from Jesus' Visitor Book

THANK YOU! I am a Christian and a lesbian and this was a beautiful expression of Faith.'s

Thank you. I want to say more soon. Somehow.

like this, I can be religious.
You brought me to tears and touched deeply.
Beautiful "show". I shall remember!!
                    Kardina

That is what a church should be for!
Enlightening, expanding, peaceful. Thankyou

Beautiful homage to life, love, wonder & humanity-
what the spiritual truly is.

Outstanding. That, in my opinion, is who
Jesus was.

Superb - Charles

Thank you! Fiona x.

Thank you.

Wonderful. Heather & Gill x

Thank you for breaking the rules
                    -Christian NEW YORK

Wonderfully moving & life affirming

Very powerful & full of (phi?) humanity
Thankyou

If church was like
this I would come
every Sunday

/so beta .

Good Church!, Roberta

The bravest thing I've seen.
Thanks for letting us be a part of it
Arabella xox

1 am from Glasgow — sorry for
how our city treated you
thank you for our blessings
Aileen x

I cannot remember the last time I felt so connected to my faith + in tune with my greatness. You made me feel so safe + so loved. Thank you. Phoebe,

Come for the bread -
stay for the spiritual rebirth.
What a joy! Simon
x

Bless you + your
Profound wisdom
Thank you.
Love + Light
Rebecca
7/8/15

ALWAYS A PLEASURE AND A PRIVILEGE TO WITNESS A PERFORMANCE WHERE THE PERFORMER ALLOWS THEMSELF TO BE AS PRESENT AS THEY CAN COME. INSPIRING x.

5th August

Thank you on behalf of every anyone who has been damaged by self-righteous religionists: and thank you so much for a deeply moving show which we all need to see, hear+take on board

That was very beautiful Thank you.

Thank you! Joyful and lovely – a wonderful message. (I also love your voice and calming presence)

More spiritual than anything I have experienced in a church.

Beautiful, uplifting, Thank you!

Also – AMAZING BREAD! Who made this??

xxx

Afterword: My Father's Hands

by Catriona Innes, journalist, novelist and daughter to Jo

Her hands look different now. They were once peppered with blue and purple varicose veins, raised just above her skin. I'd run my fingers down them, tracing these rivers with my own tiny hands. Rivers that connected directly to my dad's heart.

We used to play games. She'd hide a coin under one hand and I'd guess which by slapping quickly the hand I suspected.

It was a silly game but it kept us occupied for hours—laughing together in the café long after lunch was served.

When she transitioned, the hands I knew—so well they could almost be my own—changed with her. The veins disappeared. The skin became smooth. The pale pink nails were now painted maroon.

One day I was holding them, marvelling at how soft they were, when I noticed something: two rough, red circles right in the centre of her palms. "What are those?" I whispered. "Stigmata," she whispered back.

That was the moment I found out that my dad was Jesus.

She'd evolved once more, her hands morphing with her.

Some will say that it's just a part. An actor expertly playing a role. But those two red circles tell me otherwise. That she's here to tell us something, to teach us. She knows so much about religion—she's the only person I know who has read the Bible, front to back.

So she teaches it. To those who—at any given moment—don't feel as strong as she does. Those who see the world and its religious wars and take it as further signal that they are wrong. That they are the ones who don't belong. And my dad, Jesus, she tells them—as I sit shaking on a church pew, or perched on a red cushion in a theatre above Brighton Pier—that they are loved. Accepted. They aren't wrong at all. Together, they sob. They learn their place in the world once more.

So you can tell me that it's just a play, just a part. But you weren't there—when the stigmata began to itch on my father's hands.

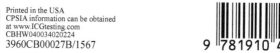

9 781910 416129